Routledge Revivals

The Teaching of Science

First published in 1969, *The Teaching of Science* primarily deals with science teaching in secondary schools and universities, but its searching discussion of criteria concerns all who have to do with education. The concise but well-documented treatments of the nature of the scientific process and of the social implications of science will be of interest to many scientists and especially useful for teachers of general studies. Professor Jevons looks first at *why* we should teach science and thereby sheds light on the more immediately practical problems of *how* it should be done. He thus does more than merely add to the already large volume of exhortation to make it more attractive and intellectually stimulating.

The Teaching of Science

Education, Science and Society

F. R. Jevons

First published in 1969
by George Allen & Unwin Ltd

This edition first published in 2022 by Routledge
4 Park Square, Milton Park, Abingdon, Oxon, OX14 4RN
and by Routledge
605 Third Avenue, New York, NY 10017

Routledge is an imprint of the Taylor & Francis Group, an informa business

© F. R. Jevons, 1969

All rights reserved. No part of this book may be reprinted or reproduced or utilised in any form or by any electronic, mechanical, or other means, now known or hereafter invented, including photocopying and recording, or in any information storage or retrieval system, without permission in writing from the publishers.

Publisher's Note
The publisher has gone to great lengths to ensure the quality of this reprint but points out that some imperfections in the original copies may be apparent.

Disclaimer
The publisher has made every effort to trace copyright holders and welcomes correspondence from those they have been unable to contact.

A Library of Congress record exists under ISBN: 0045000182

ISBN: 978-1-032-31743-4 (hbk)
ISBN: 978-1-003-31108-9 (ebk)
ISBN: 978-1-032-31744-1 (pbk)

Book DOI 10.4324/9781003311089

THE TEACHING OF SCIENCE

Education, Science and Society

BY

F. R. JEVONS

M.A., Ph.D., D.Sc.

Professor of Liberal Studies in Science
University of Manchester

London
GEORGE ALLEN AND UNWIN LTD
RUSKIN HOUSE   MUSEUM STREET

FIRST PUBLISHED IN 1969

This book is copyright under the Berne Convention. Apart from any fair dealing for the purpose of private study, research, criticism or review, as permitted under the Copyright Act, 1956, no portion may be reproduced by any process without written permission. Enquiries should be addressed to the Publishers.

© George Allen & Unwin Ltd, 1969

SBN 04 500018 2 *cloth*
SBN 04 500019 0 *paper*

PRINTED IN GREAT BRITAIN
in 11 on 12 pt. Juliana
BY THE BLACKFRIARS PRESS LTD
LEICESTER

TO JOHN AND MOLLY JEVONS

FOREWORD

This book owes a good deal to the vantage point from which I have written it. Accordingly, I would like first to express my gratitude to the University of Manchester for creating the new type of Department of which I have since 1966 been the first head. The Department of Liberal Studies in Science was set up at the initiative principally of the senior professors of physics and chemistry, B. H. Flowers and G. Gee respectively. It is responsible for a course of studies which (for reasons which are pointed out in section 4e) is known colloquially as 'Science Greats'. This undergraduate course is designed primarily to help young men and women to bring a scientific background to careers outside the laboratory (see sections 3h and 3i). The main subjects taken by students in all three years are physical science, which is taught by members of the physics, chemistry and engineering staffs, and liberal studies in science, which is defined as science looked at from the economic, social, historical and philosophical viewpoints (see section 5i). The mere fact of being in an environment in which science is looked at in these ways has naturally helped to focus my attention on the broader setting of scientific and technological education of various types.

Specific references to the activities of the Department of Liberal Studies in Science are made in note 36 to chapter 3 and in notes 13 and 38 to chapter 5. I am keenly aware of the debts I owe in many ways—for help, information, ideas, stimulation and support—to my colleagues in the Department, W. G. Evans, M. Gibbons, J. Langrish and H. Rothman. The students in the Department in the first two years of its existence have also helped me to form my views.

Further afield, I have learned a great deal from colleagues in other Departments of the Faculty of Science, in several Faculties other than Science, and in such important peripheral bodies as the Manchester University Appointments Board and the Northern Universities Joint Matriculation Board. Some names that spring to my mind are those of W. J. D. Annand, G. N. Burkhardt, A. J. Cain, D. S. L. Cardwell, J. Diamond, L. A.

Gunn, B. J. Holloway, H. S. Lipson, W. Mays, G. Murray, A. Pearson, E. H. Robinson, R. Williams and J. C. Willmott. This list is certainly not exhaustive.

I would like to thank Dr Dainton and the secretariat of his committee for allowing me to have a draft of their report before publication. Finally, I am grateful to Miss Margaret Bruce, who typed most of the manuscript, for her endearing ability to read my handwriting.

F. R. JEVONS

September 1968

CONTENTS

1	WHY TEACH SCIENCE?	page 13
2	THE NATURE OF THE SCIENTIFIC PROCESS	21
	a Progress and cumulation	21
	b The myth of infallibility	27
	c Facets of science	32
	d What makes good teaching material?	39
	e Creativity in science	44
	f Internal and external factors	49
3	THE SOCIAL IMPLICATIONS OF SCIENCE	57
	a The fundamental polarity	57
	b Galileo's campaign of cultural propaganda	61
	c Bacon's vision of science organized to give mastery over nature	65
	d The cultural value of science	73
	e Science as a way of thought	80
	f Science for material welfare	85
	g Balance between basic and applied science	88
	h Awareness of science outside the laboratory	92
	i Integrating functions	97
4	SPECIALIZATION	100
	a The nature of the problem	100
	b The lure of research	103
	c Socio-psychological considerations	106
	d Academic pressures	109
	e The meaning of depth	113
	f Arbitrariness of first degree standards	117
	g All-or-none attitudes	120
	h The ominous swing	123
	i A case for *dirigisme*?	128

5	**REFORM**	131
	a Criteria for constructing courses	131
	b Relevance to careers	133
	c A student-oriented approach	138
	d Style, not contents	139
	e The form of syllabuses	144
	f Is practical work overrated?	146
	g Integration of subject-matter	149
	h Up-to-dateness	152
	i Liberalizing science courses	154
	j Postgraduate courses	159
	k Science for non-science students	162

Notes and References   167

Index   205

CHAPTER ONE

WHY TEACH SCIENCE?

It is my intention in this book to assess the enterprise of teaching science by first examining what lies at the other end of the educational road. One cannot properly decide what is good and what is bad in education without considering its aims and purposes; and that means, in this case, looking rather hard to see what is done with science not only by scientists themselves but also by society at large. Before finding faults and preaching improvements, it is as well to consider not only how it is taught but also what it is taught for.

This is not an easy undertaking. The purposes themselves are many and complex, and the relation between means and ends is indirect. But science stands in an interestingly intermediate position here. It is neither so directly vocational that the matter is not worth discussing except in purely professional terms, nor is it so non-vocational that it is impossible to discuss except in terms of airy idealism. The answer is neither made obvious by the prospective job content, nor is it so completely elusive that it is best for the teacher to trust entirely to luck and instinct. Two cheers for luck and instinct, but also one for the clear formulation of objectives.

The importance of the task is obvious enough to need no elaboration here. Both in social and economic terms, the stakes are high. The teaching of science is expensive, and the rewards and penalties for doing it well or badly could be breath-taking. Science can easily make or break the future for mankind.

The real problem to be faced first is to analyse what success consists of. It has become fashionable in some quarters to talk about the 'cost-effectiveness' of education, and to try to assess the efficiency of the educational system by some form of input-output analysis. With regard to such attempts, there should certainly be some sympathy at least with the aim, for there is undoubtedly a good deal of misdirection of effort and underutilization of resources; but at the same time it is important not to underestimate the uncertainties. When the calculations of costs have been done—and that in itself is not as easy as it may sound, at least in the case of higher education—the biggest difficulties and the most vital issues still remain. They arise in trying to describe and define—let alone quantify—the effectiveness or benefits or output. Economists admittedly show more ingenuity than they are commonly given credit for in putting money values on things that appear not to have any. But it is necessary always to look most carefully at the criteria. Attempts with imperfect criteria could lead to plausible half-truths and thence to disaster; for while outright errors are at least liable to be detected before too long, half-truths are doubly dangerous by virtue of their insidious powers of persuasion.

Clearly it should not be the sole aim of school and university reform to maximize the output of school-leavers and graduates for given inputs of educational manpower and money. Much depends on the qualities and types of people that emerge from the educational system. But what qualities and types should we try to produce? It is hardly worth while trying to say without examining the functions they might perform, and the requirements for performing those functions well.

So the primary theme of this book is *why* we should teach natural science in our schools and universities. The more immediately practical problems of *how* it should be done are matters on which a certain amount of light should be shed in consequence. I do not want merely to add to the already large volume of exhortation to make the teaching of science more attractive and intellectually stimulating, and to supply a necessarily personal prescription for the way to set about doing it. There is no unique prescription, because there is no unique objective. The objectives are varied, and they are interrelated in complex and not always obvious ways. Hence there is liable to be confusion over the nature of the considerations that are important in designing scientific education, the criteria to be applied and the factors to be balanced. If these matters can be brought into sharper focus, the problems can at least be formulated in clearer terms, and that should go some way towards solving them.

Why Teach Science?

One obvious reason for teaching science is that a lot of scientific knowledge is available. The accumulated stock of knowledge about natural science is a significant part of the human heritage, and younger generations are given the chance to share in it by including it in accepted patterns of study in the educational system. This argument might be called the 'Mallory argument', because it boils down to the reason Mallory gave for wanting to climb Everest: 'Because it's there'. The mere existence of knowledge is taken to be a sufficient reason for teaching it.

The trouble with this line of approach is that it gives no basis for deciding between different areas of knowledge. All bits of knowledge, the implication is, are born equal and have equal rights to be taught. Some basis for choice is, however, essential, given the obvious gross disparity between the amount of knowledge available and the capacity of the human mind.

If one could summon up before the mind's eye the whole vast panorama of human knowledge, and if one could push aside all the problems of teachers, buildings, equipment and timetables (wishful thought!)—in such ideal conditions, which areas of knowledge should one choose, and on what criteria, to teach to young people at school and university?

Trying to answer this question leads immediately to an even wider one. Why teach anything at all? A question as sweeping as this is likely to get correspondingly general answers. It tends to elicit hints of man's 'highest' functions and the features that distinguish him from animals.

The suggestion of evolutionary significance here means more than might appear at first sight. Philosophers of biological evolution have read a deeper significance into the teaching process[1]. It can be said to mark a new and enormously important development in evolutionary history—not just a step in evolution, but a new departure in the evolution of evolutionary mechanism. The teaching of the young by their elders, which has been elaborated by the human species so much more than by any other, is a fresh channel through which the experience of past generations can help to shape future ones. With person-to-person learning (as in apprenticeship) supplemented by the inventions of writing and printing, a very effective mechanism has been provided for making available to new members of human society the whole accumulated knowledge and under-

The Teaching of Science

standing of the past. It amounts, in effect, to a new mode of heredity. Human young are equipped by their ancestors not only with sets of the traditional genes, shaped by millions of years of natural selection, but also with a new kind of 'genes', the facts and concepts of some two and a half millenia of scholarship.

Seen in this light, the facts and concepts of science and its ways of thought can certainly be ranked as particularly important. Since it is obvious enough that science is one of the major forces for change in the modern world, its 'genes' have particularly powerful evolutionary effects; so they form specially significant factors in the new genetics of the intellect.

Such thoughts are impressive, and help to bring home the grandeur of the whole enterprise. Perhaps it is as well, nevertheless, not to be too easily carried away by them[2]. Against the background of the vast sweep of evolutionary history, the individual might tend to get forgotten; and education has, of course, to do above all with individual people. All good education aims to promote the self-fulfilment of individuals—to draw out their innate potentialities according to the literal meaning of the word 'education'. Teachers of science in particular need to keep this fact near the surfaces of their minds, for their subject has in many quarters a reputation for being coldly objective, inhuman and impersonal. There is a story of a science teacher who forbade the use of the first person singular because he wanted 'a description of the experiment, not an autobiography'. Trivial though this anecdote is in itself, the significance of what it implies is momentous. It will be worth while later to enquire into the origins of the attitude, and its wider implications (section 2b).

One argument for teaching science might be that young people want to study it. So they do, in large numbers—but apparently the popularity of science shows some signs of declining (section 4h). Is science acquiring a public image of dullness? Do people who study it just grit their teeth and grind their way through it in the hope of something pleasant or profitable at the end?

If so, the fault can hardly lie in the subject. The idea that science in itself might be dull is just not worth considering seriously. How can there be a lack of inherent interest in one of mankind's greatest achievements—an activity which has attracted a good share of what are recognized as the greatest geniuses that the human race has produced? One could as easily argue that art and literature and music are dull. If science appears dull to students—to the extent that it might be acquiring a reputation for dullness—it *must* be the fault of those who present it badly. It is important, therefore, to try to diagnose the causes of failure (sections 2d, 5d and 5e).

The interests of individuals cannot be properly considered without reference to factors outside them. Few young people want to become hermits or pillar-saints; teachers do not in general want to produce such oddities, and educational systems are not designed to do so. Education has to be planned, therefore, with some reference to the places that those being educated might come to occupy in society and the sort of roles they might be called upon to play there.

How far it can or should go in this direction, however, remains a wide open question that requires careful examination (sections 4b, 4g, 5b). The needs of society are represented in the first instance largely by the preferences of employers, but employers' statements about them are quite liable to be ill-informed, short-sighted or misguided. The variety of possible jobs far exceeds the number of different types of education that it is practicable to provide. Even if it did not, there is a great deal that is required for career success that it is just not possible to teach, even if one were prepared to sweep aside quite ruthlessly all ideas about what constitutes a proper 'intellectual discipline'. The 'fit' or 'match' between what the educational system provides and what employers want is, therefore, at best a highly imperfect one. In specific knowledge, particular skills and general attitudes, raw school-leavers and graduates are poor approximations to ideal employees.

It is by no means self-evident, in any case, that the attempt to match education as closely as possible to prospective employment is not a misguided one. Closely matched education tends to become description of the way in which a certain function is carried out—'how it is done'. As such, it is liable to generate fixed ideas and inflexibility. By concentrating on 'how it is done' it might divert attention from 'how it might be done better'. One can easily imagine, for instance, how undergraduate courses on dough-mixing machinery or polypropylene technology might retard rather than accelerate progress in those fields, and how—

as a converse of that—people who had put all their educational eggs in those baskets might find themselves at a loss when change eventually does come, as come it must.

So the best fit between education and job content may well be a loose one; and the higher the level of the post, the looser one ought perhaps to make the fit, since higher grade posts deal with wider and less clearly defined areas. Taken to its logical—or at least extreme—conclusion, this argument would demand that the highest education should not aim at a fit at all. Universities should then take essentially no account of career opportunities in deciding what and how to teach. Ideally, they would teach only the least vocational subjects, such as history and classics, which are rather strictly non-vocational (except for the possibility of going on to teach the same subject as part of a self-perpetuating and intellectually closed system). Higher education would be purely generalist in aim, even though it might be specialist in execution, if it were judged that non-vocational specialization in history or classics is the best way to wring the educational benefits from these subjects (sections 4g, 5a). No match would then exist between education and employment except in the most generalized ways such as verbal skills in the use of language and those skills, even harder to pin down precisely, which go to make up a 'well-trained mind'. Universities would become ivory towers of scholarship and learning, quite independent of outside pressures.

This kind of view has obvious attractions and does not lack persuasive supporters, so it is as well to note an important difference between the two main lines of justification for it. On the one hand, it is said that it is pleasant for society to be able to support scholarship for its own sake, as a luxury not justified on economic grounds. Few people would take exception to this as a matter of principle, and there is room for argument only about the extent to which any given society should afford to indulge itself in this way, given that it is bound to want other expensive luxuries as well, such as fine arts or old age pensions. On the other hand, it is also said that it is best for the intellectual development of students to be immersed for a while in an environment where disinterested scholarship is paramount, sheltered from 'distortion' by external considerations and values. Here the argument is in terms of effects on students, so there

Why Teach Science?

may well be an economic or social pay-off in terms of well-trained minds emerging from the system. The *criterion* is at least partly in terms of a match between education and employment, even though the means adopted are indirect and long-term.

For the educator who is at all career-conscious on behalf of his students, science stands in a peculiar position. On the one hand, it forms a group of widely practised specialist skills on which is based a group of what are by now fairly standard professions. On the other hand, the need for education in science is not limited to the needs of these professions for recruits. The training of specialists should not be the sole objective of science teaching. It is in any case not its major function at the lower levels of the educational system, and perhaps it should not be even at the higher levels.

This consideration forms a major theme of this book. It means that to base educational provision on manpower forecasting in any narrow sense would be misguided. As a debating point, the situation is sometimes compared with teaching the three R's. It is obvious—at least in retrospect—that it would have been wrong to provide for teaching people to write only on the basis of forecasts of the number required as scribes in mediaeval monasteries or as clerks in the offices of nineteenth century capitalists. The case for teaching science is not quite the same as that for imparting the rudiments of literacy, but the differences between the two needs are probably not as great as many seem to imagine, and the value of scientific background for people not in specialized scientific occupations is something that particularly needs to be brought more into the open (sections 3h, 3i and 4h).

These are some of the problems that will have to come under scrutiny in the course of this book. What has already been said is enough to show that the purposes of science teaching fall roughly, though not neatly, under two broad heads. On the one hand, there is the demand for professional practising scientists; on the other, there is also a need for others to be educated in science. In order to help to make these two groups of objectives more specific and to state them in more detailed ways, chapters 2 and 3 examine respectively the nature of the scientific process itself and the wider social implications of science.

When that has been done, however, the task is not over. However clear the objectives can be made, the ways and means to achieve them do not automatically become obvious. Since the relation between educational means and ends is usually indirect, and often very much so, it may be best in many cases not to aim too specifically at what appears to be the target. Roundabout ways may turn out to be the most effective ones.

The educator himself is—or should be—the real expert here. It is up to him to balance the factors and arrive at appropriate educational solutions. Accordingly, chapters 4 and 5 make an attempt to work out in educational terms some of the complex implications of the analyses of chapters 2 and 3.

CHAPTER TWO

THE NATURE OF THE SCIENTIFIC PROCESS

a. PROGRESS AND CUMULATION

A good way to start to examine the nature of the scientific process may be to ask what it is that is special about it. What is unique, or at least distinctive, about science when compared with other human activities? A number of possible answers may spring to mind; some of them may seem obvious at first sight but turn out on closer scrutiny to need a great deal of hedging about with qualifications. There is one, however, which seems to me to be both outstandingly simple and outstandingly significant. It is this—that science has made *progress* in a sense which is clearer and less disputable than is the case with other fields of human endeavour.

This is not a proposition that can be proved, since there is no quantitative measure of progress whose validity it is not easy to question. One can, however, add substance and conviction to the assertion by means of an imaginary operation or 'thought-experiment' suggested by Conant. 'Bring back to life the great figures of the past who were identified with the subjects in question. Ask them to view the present scene and answer whether or not in their opinion there has been an advance'[1]. Take Kepler, Galileo or Newton—there can be no doubt how they would reply after a guided tour of a modern physics laboratory. The verdicts of Boyle and Harvey on modern chemistry and biology are just as predictable. But in fields outside science, judgments would be much more debatable. Suppose we could bring back some more figures from the seventeenth century—Richelieu to assess politics, Descartes or Locke for philosophy, Rembrandt for painting, Monteverdi or Purcell for music, Wren for architecture. It is true, of course, that spokesmen for the twentieth century could put quite good cases to them. They could argue, for instance — and with quite reasonable justification — that politics nowadays is greater in scope, subtlety and sophistication; that philosophy can boast of a rigour of formal logic and a fineness of verbal discrimination previously unknown; that paintings and music have reached unprecedented complexity of expression and penetrated new areas of imagination; that modern buildings use forms of a size, a sweep and a daring to which earlier architects could not aspire. But when all that has been said, the cases remain far from clear-cut. The verdicts are at least not self-evident. The mere fact that fascinating debate rather than instant conviction is the likely outcome is in itself enough to prove the point.

Of course there are fringe areas where doubt remains as to whether they belong with the sciences or the non-sciences. But there is no need here to embark on any demarcation disputes about them. The main and crucial fact stands out quite clearly—that in the typical natural sciences the fact of genuine and substantial progress is beyond reasonable doubt, whereas in typical non-sciences it is not.

This simple fact of progress already achieved is a significant one. It lies at the root of a number of important things both about the practice of science by professional scientists and about the teaching of science to students. So it is worth enquiring a little into the reasons behind it. Why and how has science succeeded in progressing?

Clearly, it would not have succeeded so well if it had not managed to make itself *cumulative* in a very effective way. For progress to be sustained generation after generation, scientists must often be able to start where their predecessors left off. Of course there are plenty of false starts up blind alleys—science is not, when one looks closely, a steady and inexorable march forward — but individual scientists do not each have to start afresh from the beginning; if they did, none of them would ever get very far. In a developed branch of science, every worker stands on the shoulders of a long line of intellectual ancestors. Newton remarked that, if he had been able to see further than others, it was because he stood on the shoulders of giants. The same applies all the more to modern scientists—with only the proviso that non-giants can also help.

The Nature of the Scientific Process

The potentiality for cumulation can be partly explained by characteristics inherent in the subject-matter. The subject-matter of the typical natural sciences was there centuries ago, is here now and continues to remain with us. This enables us to go on studying the same thing further and further, making more extensive and more detailed observations, setting up more searching experiments to probe deeper and deeper. Scientists in laboratories accept the uniformity of nature as a fact, leaving it to philosophers to argue about the justification. Heavy bodies still fall in the same way as in Galileo's time, the reactions of sulphuric acid remain unchanged and so does the way the blood circulates in animal bodies. The subject-matter of natural science does not recede and become attenuated as does that of history, nor is it as obviously mutable and impermanent as is much of that of social studies.

The permanent availability of the subject-matter does not, however, by itself explain the cumulative nature of the scientific process. It may be a necessary condition but is not a sufficient one. The subject-matter was, after all, available to the earliest human civilizations, but history shows that it is only within the last few centuries that science has so effectively made itself cumulative. There must be something important in the mode of the enquiry as well as in its matter.

In that something, a principal factor is the fact that science has been able to establish powerful research traditions. Such traditions exercise strong guiding influences on the direction of scientific effort and the way in which scientific work is carried out. Among the scientists operating within a tradition, there is a large measure of agreement about the kinds of problems that can usefully be tackled and about fruitful ways of tackling them. A tradition is established when scientists in substantial numbers base themselves on a common heritage of earlier work. From this earlier work is derived a set of models on the basis of which further work can be patterned and planned; certain types of experiment, techniques of analysis and so on become standard in the field. Thus sets of scientists come to adopt—even if only implicitly—substantial sets of common assumptions and attitudes.

The basic, broad research traditions are associated with the establishment of key concepts. To a large extent, indeed, the

The Teaching of Science

traditions of problem-type and mode of approach are embodied in such key concepts. Mechanics, for instance, is based largely on the notions of inertia, mass, force and acceleration, chemistry on those of elements, atoms and molecules, biology on those of classification, cells and evolution. These have shown themselves to be fruitful since a great deal of constructive work has been done with them; they form conceptual frameworks which have been tried, proved and found useful in gathering and ordering knowledge and in solving problems. More limited and more detailed research traditions arise within the broad ones, of course —traditions of work in X-ray crystallography, for instance, or of nutritional research such as that which led to the discovery and isolation of vitamins.

The existence of long and highly developed traditions is not just a fact about the intellectual and social structure of science; it has important practical consequences as well. It helps, for instance, to account for the barriers of exclusiveness that have arisen around scientific work. Scientists form an 'in-group'—or rather, a whole series of in-groups, one should say, in order to avoid the over-simplification that there are only two cultures. There is an element of the 'closed shop' about science, however little those on the inside want it.

Patterns of communication show this fact up well. Partly as a cause, partly as an effect, communication of much scientific information has come to take place along increasingly restricted channels. This trend began during that period in the seventeenth and eighteenth centuries in which modern science began to gather momentum. This was the period which saw the beginning of the replacement of books by research papers as the normal and dominant way of publishing research results[2]. Instead of writing books in which the subject was developed more or less from scratch, scientists began to publish papers aimed at fellow-workers in the field. By now, the research paper has developed to the stage where, apart from a brief introduction—often no more than a gesture—the background is often given only in the form of references to earlier published papers. It would be possible in theory to dig out this background by following the reference citations back through a number of 'generations' of published papers, building up a lengthy scientific genealogy. In practice, of course, nobody ever bothers to do this at all fully;

The Nature of the Scientific Process

even for the specialist, there are easier ways of reading up the background. But the background is there all the same, and its weight is such—there is such an accumulation of facts and theories, techniques, conventions, symbols, vocabulary (not to say jargon)—that the contents of a typical research paper are properly accessible only to a limited group. The group may, of course, be widely spread geographically, but it is often quite small in number.

The research paper is therefore both an expression of, and a vehicle for, the growth of specialization. One may bemoan the fragmentation of knowledge that it implies, but it would be burying one's head in the sand to deny that it (or some equivalent) is necessary. Without it, efficient cumulation would not be possible. Take an example simplified to near-absurdity: imagine the state of chemistry if every author of every chemical paper had to explain and justify all that he assumes or takes for granted, from the existence of atoms onwards. Chemistry would be crippled.

Much of the background can be condensed, organized, rationalized and presented in the form of lectures, textbooks, reviews and so on; but important components of it do not lend themselves to this kind of processing. These get buried and go underground; they become 'tacit' rather than 'explicit' knowledge (to use the words with meanings that are related to, though not identical with, those given them by Polanyi[3]). The existence of such components has important repercussions on the training of research workers; it accounts, at least in large part, for the almost universal institution of a kind of apprenticeship in research. The special significance of this is considered further below (section 2c).

Even away from the research front, the existence of large accumulations of background means that science is not freely accessible to laymen. Any educated person can reasonably expect to be able to make something of most of the output of historians, but the same cannot be said of most of the output of scientists. Anyone who wants to get genuine access to science has to bind himself to a formidable and prolonged novitiate. The intellectual entrance fee to the scientific group of clubs is high.

For the teaching of science, both at school and at undergraduate level, this constitutes both an incentive and a barrier.

The Teaching of Science

It means that science has a success story to tell, but that the telling is difficult. It means that science can offer a special kind of reward, in the status that expertise brings with it; but that at the same time it runs the risk of smothering itself in the abundance of its own growth.

A special challenge that faces science teaching is, therefore, to devise suitable short cuts through the accumulation of knowledge that has been built up. In saying this, I do not wish to imply that as science progresses it necessarily piles up pedagogic difficulties in proportion. Advances in theory may serve to ease rather than aggravate the teaching problem. Grand generalizations come to unify and structure large bodies of information; the increasing power of theory to organize facts makes for intellectual economy and lightens the burden on students and teachers. But this does not, on the whole, reverse the trend (section 4d). One must not forget, after all, that the sophistication of the theory involved, its own inherent intellectual difficulty, itself tends to increase.

So there is a special responsibility which should be borne in mind by all who are concerned with scientific education: to make sure that science does not pay the penalty of its own success by pricing itself out of the intellectual market. It seems that in many countries there has set in, during the last few

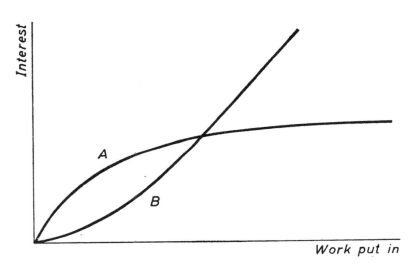

years, a swing against scientific studies (section 4h). The causes are certainly many and complex, but it does seem probable that the apparent initial difficulties of scientific subjects are among them. Some people have it that subjects fall into two classes according to the way that interest changes with the amount of work put in. Type A generates high interest in the early stages but the rate of return soon drops off; in type B there is a lag phase before take-off begins. If there is any truth in this analysis, obvious oversimplification though it is, then it means that, where subject choices are available, there are bound to be forces pulling in the direction of type A, especially among those who do not feel irrevocably committed to lifelong devotion to the subjects they study in their youth. That being the case, it is all the more important not to accept the analysis fatalistically as an unchangeable fact of nature. The early part of curve B *can* be pushed upwards.

b. THE MYTH OF INFALLIBILITY

Having, in the last section, insisted on the great and genuine progress that science has achieved, it is time now to insist equally strongly that this does not mean that it automatically and inevitably reaches correct conclusions. The fact that advances have been made does not mean that the possibility of error has been eliminated. Success is not the same as infallibility. Yet there are many people who appear to think that, short of sheer incompetence, science is always right. G. K. Chesterton even thought it a mere truism to say that 'physical science is like simple addition: it is either infallible or it is false'[4]. The same is implied by much popular usage of the word 'scientific'. One might hear, for instance, that hair restorer of brand X has been 'scientifically' proved to work better than brand Y. The idea seems to be that all a competent scientist ever does is to employ some sure means of drawing certain conclusions by unerring reason from indisputable facts.

The myth of infallibility is important because it is prevalent, and it is potentially dangerous because it can lead to unwarranted dogmatism not only in but also about science. If science had discovered some methodological philosopher's stone, some guaranteed way of arriving at right answers, then one would not want to miss the opportunity of applying it to other areas of human activity. It would be right to try to generate some methodological 'fall-out' or 'spin-off' as a side-benefit that society could derive from science. Given, however, that scientific method is not infallible, it is not hard to see dangers not very deeply hidden in such attempts. It is not only the transferability of method from one area of enquiry to another that is in question, but also the complete trustworthiness of the method in the first place.

As a matter of fact, among academic disciplines, attempts to ape science—and especially physical science—are already quite a time-honoured activity, and it is possible to see that the blessings they have brought have not been unmixed. Even within the field of natural science, one can see that the application of the physical science approach to the problems of biology, although it has made possible enormous strides forward, has also, when uncritical, led to misdirection of effort[5]. The same can be said, with perhaps even more justification, of various kinds of social studies, which sometimes seem over-anxious to emulate the quantitative and mathematical aspect of physical science.

It is especially where academic interests impinge on the practical conduct of human affairs that misconceptions about methodology could lead to unwelcome consequences. Here it is worth distinguishing between two different kinds of situation— that where scientists themselves get too big for their boots and that where non-scientists show a touching but exaggerated faith in the power of scientific method. The former is, of course, a tradition well established in fiction of varying degrees of seriousness; the scientist who believes he holds an easy key to the world's problems, indulges in power-dreams and eventually tries to put them into effect is almost a stock figure. But it is the latter type of situation, where non-scientists try to apply what they believe to be scientific method to the problems facing them, which may well be the more dangerous one.

Let me illustrate this rather vague and general point by referring to a particular case. There is a book by Gilpin called *American Scientists and Nuclear Weapons Policy* which is of interest in that it tries not only to tell the story but also to generalize and codify the principles underlying the relations between scientists and politicians. Gilpin argues that American

The Nature of the Scientific Process

scientists have tried to solve each political problem by the 'logic of the facts', that they have looked for an objective answer to each problem, a unique correct solution. He says that 'much of the history of the politics of scientists since 1945 has been a search for such objective answers to political problems . . . solutions based on facts and, therefore, acceptable to all'[6].

Undoubtedly there is some justification for this verdict, but it is possible to show that the converse has also happened. In so far as the errors have been methodological ones, scientists have not been either universally or exclusively guilty of them.

As an outstanding example of advice by scientists on a political issue, one might take the Franck Report[7]. This was drawn up by seven eminent scientists who had been working on the development of the atomic bomb, and it was sent to the Secretary for War in June 1945, one month before the first atomic test explosion at Los Alamos. In its text, it is difficult to see any insistence by the scientists on a unique objective solution. After giving facts known at the time to few outsiders (for obvious reasons), they weigh the possible courses of action, taking into account such imponderables as international trust and mass psychology.

By contrast, one might cite a publication of political origin, the U.S. Department of State's *Report on the International Control of Atomic Energy*. Issued in 1946, this contained the Acheson-Lilienthal proposals for an international agency to control uranium production. Lilienthal said that his committee had had 'an opportunity to analyze what is called a political problem in a scientific spirit . . . We started somewhat as a chemist might, tackling a technical problem with the facts as he found them . . . We have described the process whereby we arrived at our recommendation, to make it clear that we did not begin with a preconceived plan . . . Others would have a similar experience if they were able to go through a period of close study of the alternatives and an absorption in the salient and determining facts'[8].

It is quite clear what kind of view of scientific method is being assumed here. It is a view according to which science starts from facts and leads to unique, objective solutions. Of course this kind of view is popular, but it is not shared by many of those who have thought most deeply about the matter. The point is one that seems worth taking up here, because it is not just a philosophical point of purely academic interest. It has practical implications, too. An understanding of the nature of the scientific process that is as clear and as accurate as possible is important because of its relevance to the question of the possible transfer of successful methodology to other fields (which in turn is connected with the educational value of science for careers in fields not strictly scientific). People who are going to copy science must beware of copying the wrong thing about it. If science has a formula for success, the prescription must not be misread.

In considering scientific method, perhaps the simplest antithesis that it is useful to make is between the inductive and the hypothetico-deductive points of view. According to the inductive scheme (often but rather misleadingly called 'Baconian'—see section 3c), the scientist collects facts with an entirely open and unprejudiced mind, then inspects the facts and determines the laws governing them by induction. This view has stood for some three centuries now as what might well be called the standard naïve philosophy of scientific method. Its great virtue has seemed to be the way it emphasizes the reliance that science places on empirical facts. Constant appeal to them, ungrudging acceptance of their role as ultimate arbiters of validity and truth, has been seen as the way to dispel the mists of primitive superstition and ignorance, to break the fetters of outworn authorities and traditions and to avoid the philosophical hair-splitting and in-fighting that were the worst aspects of the mediaeval scholasticism out of which modern science grew.

The simple inductive scheme seems to many, however, to give a misleading picture of the relation of theory to empirical facts. It is impossible, the argument runs, to collect and inspect facts with an entirely empty mind. One always has *some* kind of expectation in advance with which one approaches the facts. So, according to the hypothetico-deductive view, the scientist guesses at some hypothesis, deduces the consequences and checks them against the observed facts. If there is agreement, the hypothesis is corroborated; if not, it is refuted.

The role of empirical facts in this scheme, while comparable in importance, is different in kind. Facts function less as direct originators of theories than as tests of them. The means by which hypotheses are arrived at remains a more or less complete mystery. Words like guess, hunch, intuition or inspiration serve

The Nature of the Scientific Process

to give it a label but not to tell one much about it. Thus a crucial role is reserved for an irrational element in science.

The importance of this non-logical, irrational component has been emphasized in various ways by a number of important modern writers. Polanyi, for instance, has done so in his book, *Personal Knowledge*[9], which is unfortunately too long and too difficult for many people to have read. Koestler, too, has made similar points in books which are also too long but perhaps not difficult enough to be taken as seriously as they otherwise might be. The title of *The Sleepwalkers* indicates his view of outstanding scientists, and his analysis of *The Act of Creation* emphasizes the subjective and irrational aspect it has in science as well as in humour and in art[10].

Notably, too, there is Popper[11], in whose hands the hypothetico-deductive philosophy has developed into the principle of falsifiability. Observations, Popper argues, can falsify or refute a hypothesis and show it to be definitely wrong; but a theory can never be conclusively proved correct because tests can never be exhaustive and the possibility always remains of a new and better hypothesis. This leads him to the conclusion that there can never be real certainty about scientific theories. Far from being the logical outcome of facts—not even conclusively verifiable by facts—they are really conjectures, often intellectually daring conjectures; and science progresses by criticizing them and replacing them when refuted.

In the writings of these authors, different though they are in many ways, one common basic theme can be detected. None of them will admit that detached objectivity which has often been supposed to be the hallmark that distinguishes scientists from the rest of mankind and science from other human ventures. To that extent, they could be said to be working towards a 'reunification of culture', a breaking of the barriers between a supposedly impersonal, coldly factual and logical science on the one hand and imaginative, creative, open-ended activities of the human mind on the other.

With any such attempt, there is bound to be widespread sympathy. But the mere fact that it has to be made poses a problem for us. If it is true that science is really a major exploit of the human imaginative and creative faculties, why does it suffer so widely from a very different public image? Why is it that so

The Teaching of Science

many people think of science as just mountains of dull, dry facts held together (if at all) by impeccable but unexciting logic?

To understand this, it is necessary to analyse the scientific process a little further, and also to examine some features of the teaching process. I believe that it can be shown that a large part of the explanation can be found in the indirectness of the relation between science as it is practised and science as it is taught. Certain peculiarities of the educational process almost inevitably introduce distortions of a particular kind. It may not be possible or even desirable to avoid the distortions altogether, but it is as well at least to be aware of their existence and their nature so that one realizes what one is doing.

c. FACETS OF SCIENCE

We must at this stage clarify our ideas about what science really is. This involves plunging into rather deeper philosophical waters and it will be as well, therefore, to say briefly right at the outset what the burden of the argument is. It is that a distinction should be drawn between the knowledge that is a product of science and the process by which it is acquired. This distinction is neither abstruse nor trivial. Failure to make it has led to the prevalence of views which are deficient in important ways and whose existence helps to account for some of the apparent conflicts of opinions that one encounters regarding science. That is why the matter is worth developing here more fully.

If one were to conduct a sort of opinion poll among reasonably well-informed and thoughtful people to find out what they consider science to be, many of the answers would probably be in line with Herbert Spencer's definition: 'science is organized knowledge'. This accords well with the etymological derivation of the word, which comes from the Latin word *scientia*, meaning knowledge or wisdom. Natural science is then organized knowledge about the natural world—the multitude of known facts about the universe, linked together by theory, which serves to co-ordinate, arrange and systematize them. Science is seen as a very full and powerful description of nature. Essentially, it is an enormously developed version of the story about nature that Plato told twenty-three centuries ago in his *Timaeus*—vastly filled out in detail, of course, and with far greater verisimilitude,

The Nature of the Scientific Process

achieved through the long process of critical checking and testing against nature empirically observed, but still recognizably in the same tradition of 'nature-stories' as the famous Greek prototype.

Science as it is written in many books, perhaps the majority of books, conforms pretty well to this view (cf. also section 5e). My purpose here is to show, however, that it is inadequate and misleading in some important respects.

A step in the direction of a fuller and more representative view is taken in the definition given recently by the distinguished members of the Committee on Manpower Resources for Science and Technology. They define the sciences as 'an interlocking complex of attested fact and speculative theory, with the essential proviso that theories must be capable of being tested experimentally'[12]. The important thing here is the emphasis on testing. This testing and all that it involves is actually just as essential to science as the facts and theories. Science, indeed, is not just a body of knowledge but a process of inquiry. In this process, the nature-story plays an important part, but it is no more than just one part of what goes to make up the total process.

To avoid the danger of getting embroiled in an argument that turns only on semantics—a discussion of what different people mean when they use the word 'science'—it may be useful to take an operational definition of the word. Let us say that science is what practising scientists are professionally concerned with—surely that does not seem unreasonable—and see what kind of picture of science can be developed on that basis.

With this starting-point, it does not take long to reach the conclusion that science is far from exclusively concerned with facts and theories about nature. Other aspects of the scientific process occupy most of the time and energy of scientists. The layman would be wrong to think that, when scientists in a laboratory are 'talking shop', they talk mostly about 'nature-story' topics like the behaviour of subatomic particles or of molecules or of cells. He would be even more wrong to think that topics of other kinds are merely minor details of secondary importance.

Notably, among such other topics, are included questions of technique, apparatus and instrumentation. The history of science abounds with examples of discoveries that were easy to make once problems of technique had been solved, and many of the practising scientists of today could add a few from their personal experiences. Hence the scientific profession rightly sets high store by technique in its own right. Outsiders often fail to realize how highly sheer technique is valued relative to results. To help to convince them, one might point to Nobel prizes awarded for development of techniques rather than 'nature-story' discoveries; the 1952 award to Martin and Synge for partition chromatography is an outstanding example. The hardware of research plays not only an enabling but also a directive role. It makes some things possible and others impracticable; the facts of its existence and availability, its foibles, potentialities and limitations are often crucial. It just will not do to dismiss them by taking a high and mighty Platonic line and pretending that the intellectual process—the operation of the minds of scientists on facts and theories—is all that really counts in governing the pace and direction of scientific advance.

At least as important as the hardware is the 'software' which also surrounds the facts and theories of the nature-story. With this I include the background of assumptions made explicitly or tacitly taken for granted; the method of approach, the way of seeing the problem-structure of a field and isolating individual problems from it; and ideas about the types of answers to be sought, which may differ widely at different times or according to external circumstances which set up different criteria of desirability for the solutions to be aimed at (most obviously and crudely, between pure and applied science, but also according to differences which are subtler but just as real). The 'knack' of the successful scientist, his 'feel' for research, depend as much on his ability to manipulate this complex of intangibles as on his mastery of technique.

Indeed, it is here that originality emerges from mere competence. It shows itself in the scientist's choices of problems to work on and of lines of attack on them. These are neither obvious nor predetermined. They depend on judgments as to what is worth doing and the likelihood of being able to do it; just as with many decisions outside science, what counts is the value of a given achievement times the probability of success in achieving it, and—again as is common outside science—neither of these inputs into the decision-making process can normally be

The Nature of the Scientific Process

evaluated without relying on personal judgments. Scientists see no virtue or credit in working on a problem of outstanding interest or importance unless there seems to be a reasonable chance of solving it. As Medawar has it, science is 'the art of the soluble'[13] and this helps to explain, incidentally, even if it does not necessarily excuse, the fact that so much scientific work seems pointless or misdirected to outsiders.

It is in connection with this kind of software that research traditions play specially important roles. It is not at all easy, it is true, to pin down and describe specifically in words the precise forms they take and the exact ways in which they operate. But this very difficulty is perhaps the most important thing about them. Since it is not easy to state them explicitly, they are not public and open knowledge in quite the same way that the facts and theories of the nature-story are. Because of the tacit components of traditions, they are learned not so much by reading books or listening to lectures as by actually doing some research with collaboration and guidance by more experienced workers.

These characteristics inherent in the nature of the scientific process reflect themselves quite clearly in the social organization that science has developed for itself. They form the basis and justification for the kind of apprenticeship which figures almost universally in the training of research workers. Budding scientists learn their trade by working for a time in close and active contact with an established research worker. Normally the years as research student working for a Ph.D. form the apprenticeship period, and the research supervisor fulfils the role of master to the apprentice. There is an important craft element in the practice of research, and the existence of a certain amount of craft 'mystery' reflects itself in this degree of parallelism between the institutional structures of modern science and mediaeval craft guilds. (Indeed, the parallelism could easily be taken a step further, for the modern research fellow corresponds quite well to the mediaeval journeyman.)

At one level, the high level of outstanding research workers, the importance of the teacher-pupil relationship in science is shown in those scientific genealogies which emphasize the seminal roles played by key individuals on subsequent work through their pupils over several generations. Thus 16 Nobel laureates are 'descended' from von Baeyer, and more than 30 from Liebig. From a discussion of these and other cases, Krebs[14] concludes that 'how to select worthwhile problems and how to create the tools required to achieve a solution is something that scientists learn from the great figures in science rather than from books'.

In a more overall sense, the same factor may well underlie the observed fact that the growth of science, as indicated by any of a number of sufficiently large-scale measures, has been roughly exponential. To the extent that new workers have to go through an apprenticeship, rather than just learning facts and theories which can be read by anybody anywhere, their number should be proportional to the number of workers already established; that is, the rate of growth should vary as the existing size at any given time. This could well help to explain the tendency for growth to continue exponentially as long as external constraints, in the form of limitations on manpower or money, do not make themselves felt. The overall doubling time of 10 to 15 years pointed out by Price[15] seems quite a reasonable one if one thinks of reasonable values for the time-lag for apprentices to become masters, the apprentice to master ratio, and losses through death and change of occupation. Indeed, the indications are that purely internal factors work towards exponential growth of any sector of science, and the implication is that a policy for science of unlimited support and *laissez-faire* would in fact produce this result in most sectors, with doubling periods varying appreciably on both sides of the above figures but mostly of the same order of magnitude.

Having now briefly sketched some aspects of a picture of the scientific process, it is time to state and answer a type of objection that might be raised against it with some appearance of justification. It could be said that I have taken altogether too professional a view of the matter—that, in emphasizing the importance of facets of science other than facts and theories about nature, I have become too deeply involved with the means and not kept them separate enough from the ends. Could the elements that I have described as hardware and software perhaps be dismissed as mere accessories that should not be elevated to the same status as the nature-story knowledge which is the guiding purpose of the whole enterprise? Perhaps they are merely the mechanism behind the scenes with which the practising specialist has per-

The Nature of the Scientific Process

force to come to grips but which is of little concern to anyone else. Have I confused the backstage activity with the play? Or scientific research with just 'science'—knowledge that can just be known and used? Why should not the majority of us gratefully accept the results without bothering unduly about the process by which they were obtained?

In one or two important respects at least, there are good reasons why we should not, lest from misleading impressions about the way science functions we form false conclusions about the way in which it can or should be handled, particularly as regards its propagation and transmission. If the relation of the scientific process to the nature-story were merely that of productive process to finished article, the significance of the former would be limited to and exhausted by the completion of the latter; but it is not, and in this respect science differs from, say, the production of manufactured articles like saucepans or screws, where most people are quite content to use the product and leave it to production engineers to worry about processes of manufacture. In the cases of saucepans and screws, this is reprehensible only to the extent that any limitation of curiosity and inquisitiveness is reprehensible (and they cannot, after all, profitably be universal). But in the case of science there is a good deal more to be said against it than in the cases of saucepans or screws. In considering science as a social force active in various ways, or in discussing the training of scientists, or science as a component of general education, it is a very poor approximation to take science as tantamount to nature-story. The other facets of science — roughly and broadly speaking, its methodological components — are at least as important.

It is useful, I think, to view the relation of scientific process to nature-story not so much as that of productive process to finished article as that of concrete to abstraction. Concrete, according to the relevant dictionary definition, is 'a term applied to an object as it exists in nature, invested with all its attributes'. By abstraction we isolate for separate consideration some of the things or qualities that are united in a complex concrete object. If science is here the 'object' that exists in nature, then concrete science consists of actual scientific achievements, with all the many and complex factors that go into their making. The nature-story is one particular pattern of abstraction that can be made from this; it is formed by taking and putting together the bits of information about the physical world, in the form of facts and theories, that constitute one type of item that goes into the make-up of concrete achievements. (It may be worth mentioning that this treatment in terms of concrete and abstraction is based on Whitehead's famous Fallacy of Misplaced Concreteness[16]. My argument could be summed up by saying that it is a fallacy of misplaced concreteness to equate the nature-story with science.)

Let me now point to some ways in which the view that the nature-story can be taken to represent science turns out to be clearly deficient. If science is defined as what scientists are concerned with, then a parallel operational definition is to say that its product is what they produce. Now the primary products of scientists, it is quite clear, are research papers. If one examines the contents of such papers, one finds that they are not exclusively or even predominantly concerned with facts and theories about nature. In representative cases, they deal mostly with experimental details, descriptions of materials and methods; many are devoted entirely to matters of technique. Yet, despite this, there can be no doubt that they are highly valued items in the scientific scheme of things. They are often said to constitute scientific property—or rather, their publication is said to be the accepted way for scientists to assert and guard the property rights to which they feel entitled over their original work. The regular occurrence of priority disputes and the bitterness they frequently engender have been held to indicate the major role that such property rights play in the motivation of scientists[17]. Publications have been used as a measure of scientific productivity[18], and a scientist's promotion prospects, as well as his prestige among his peers, depend largely on their number and quality.

The veneration of research papers may be contrasted, on the other hand, with a relative disdain of nature-story, as represented typically by books. The activity of actually writing nature-story tends to be less highly valued, within science at least, than the production of research papers. Scientists who set out to produce good pictures of substantial parts of nature by writing books find that as a result their stock among their fellow-scientists is as likely to go down as up. This fact has also been noted by Kuhn[19] and it is of some interest, since it seems that in this respect the scientific environment differs from what is usual in the arts faculties of universities.

To this it may be objected that the relatively low valuation of books as compared to research papers is due to the fact that new scientific information nowadays is rarely published for the first time in books, and that research papers are in fact judged for quality by the contribution that they make to nature-story knowledge. Occasionally, it is true, it is said that the real test of the value of a contribution is whether it gets included in textbooks for students. Such criteria seem, however, to be applied relatively seldom. Research tends to be judged by the criteria of research, not by those of textbook writers.

Another important shortcoming of equating science with nature-story is that it fails to represent adequately the dynamic continuity of science. Science is a cumulative and self-propagating process. A good piece of scientific work is not a cul-de-sac; it may raise new problems (or at least leave loose ends) or it may indicate new means with which to attack old problems. In such ways, impetus is maintained and one piece of work leads on to others. When an 'apprentice'—a research student—is initiated into science in the concrete, he comes to see problems as well as achievements; indeed, the most important aspect of his apprenticeship is that he should learn to see new problems of a manageable kind in conjunction with ways of tackling them. Mere items in the description of nature, however, do not do this —they do not lead on to anything beyond themselves. Merely to say that DNA is a double helix of such and such dimensions, or to state the electronic configurations of atoms, suggests nothing—neither ways of testing the validity of the statements nor further developments from them, either experimental or theoretical. The abstracted facts and theories about nature are, by themselves, a sterile kind of knowledge; only concrete science is fertile in the sense that it is capable of leading on to yet further knowledge.

d. WHAT MAKES GOOD TEACHING MATERIAL?

This brings us to the most glaring of all the deficiencies of the view that science can be taken to be just nature-story—one that manifests itself below the research level in the teaching of science at school and in university courses and is therefore particularly relevant to the subject of this book. Nature-story, bare and unadorned, makes dull and uninspiring teaching material. Consider some examples: the equation for the period of a pendulum, the atomic numbers of carbon and oxygen, the formulae of potassium permanganate and acetic acid, the structure of the mammalian heart. Merely to learn these by themselves would represent all that is anathema to the progressive spirit in education. Students forced to do it would soon complain—and justifiably—of having to learn by rote, merely to regurgitate the memorized material later.

Yet all the examples I have mentioned are, beyond doubt, important and significant ones in the description of nature. They certainly do not lack potential interest; the problem of making good teaching material out of them is the problem of making this potential interest actual for students. The way to do this can be put in general terms on the basis of the preceding discussion as follows: that it is to invest them with some elements of 'concreteness'. This can be done by placing them in the context of something more like a real scientific situation. It need not necessarily be a time-slice of authentic research, but it should resemble it to the extent of possessing a measure of the intellectual dynamism of the process. One could consider, for instance, how the information was or might be obtained, what kind of conjectures, assumptions, observations or reasoning could lead to it, what is the nature of the evidence supporting it, what other information it ties up with. Or one could ask what can be done with it once one has got it, whether it can be used for finding out other things or how it can be made the basis of practical applications.

In short, if one tries to interpret with reference to science the theme that Whitehead developed in *The Aims of Education*[20]—that teaching should not consist of merely handing on dead knowledge and inert ideas—it amounts to this: that one must present not only a description of nature but also something of the other elements of concrete scientific situations.

This is not, unfortunately, the kind of prescription that leads easily to a panacea for all the aches and pains of science teaching. It merely states the problem in what I believe to be a potentially useful form. It is based on a counterpart of the distinction I have

The Nature of the Scientific Process

drawn between sterile and fertile knowledge at the research level. Just as dead nature-story cannot lead on to further research, so it is also incapable of generating fruitful activity in the minds of students. The proposition that 'activity is the only road to knowledge', which for Bernard Shaw was a 'maxim for revolutionists', is now little more than a piece of the conventional wisdom of educationists, and so the job of the teacher becomes clear, in general terms at least. It is to invest items in the description of nature with enough of the other facets of situations in a scientific process to give the minds of students a chance to operate actively on the material.

The difficulty of doing this may be brought out by considering some of the kinds of approach that are sometimes suggested. The 'find-out-for-yourself' approach sounds superficially attractive; it may seem at first sight to meet the requirements as fully as it is possible to do so. In practice, it depends very much on how the slogan is interpreted. If it means finding out for yourself by looking and experimenting, or even by thinking and reasoning, then it does rather underestimate the difficulties. Not only does it slow down the pace at which ground can be covered (that penalty is one that is worth paying, up to a limit, if the educational objectives of awakening curiosity, sharpening wits, deepening understanding and developing judgment and self-confidence are achieved); but it also restricts the scope of what can be done and creates at least the risk that topics that are difficult to treat in this way may tend to be avoided. If, on the other hand, the implication is that students should be encouraged to find out for themselves by using books and articles instead of relying on the teacher, then it touches on a point that may be worth taking quite seriously as one where the teaching of science compares in a needlessly unfavourable way with what is common practice in other subjects (sections 5d to 5f).

Backing up all assertions by describing the supporting evidence—which is, in a sense, a second-hand version of the find-out-for-yourself approach—is also something that can easily be overdone. It is just not true that good science consists of taking nothing for granted. Students, like researchers, have to learn to take a great deal for granted. If they were not prepared to do this, cumulation would be impossible. If everybody insisted on questioning everything, demanding rigorous proofs of every mathematical manipulation and tests of every chemical technique, refusing to use instruments as black boxes without a full understanding of their inner circuitry, it would be less likely that anybody would ever get around to focusing attention on new issues and asking the new questions that need to be asked. Of course it is true that many big steps forward have come from doubting what had hitherto been unquestioningly accepted; but the healthy and fruitful kind of scepticism is selective, not universal.

Similarly, it would be wrong to put too much reliance on the historical approach. I say this despite my firm conviction that the history of science holds immense educational potentialities which are crying out to be exploited and which we have barely begun to tap (section 5k). We should certainly put more effort into this field, but there are good and bad ways of setting about it. Any history is not necessarily better than none. There is little to be said, for instance, in favour of adding a snippet of history to every topic. Those historical introductions of the textbooks, the odd historical references at the beginnings of chapters, are usually awful. Only exceptionally do they succeed in doing much to deepen understanding of an important point. Rarely based on first-hand historical study, they sometimes amount merely to the dropping of a few illustrious names; or they may take the form of anecdotes chosen—all too often—more for romantic appeal than for accuracy. Such gestures tend to be ignored by beginners and to irritate those who know. They do little more than to discredit the historical approach.

In the case of chemistry there was, even quite recently, an appreciable historical content in elementary courses, but this has largely disappeared now and there is not much reason to mourn its passing. School-leavers, it was sometimes said, remembered more about phlogiston than about atoms, and to return to such a state of affairs is hardly the way to solve our problems. Undergraduates in many subjects have for years cursed lecturers who, out of an entirely mistaken sense of duty, wasted the first lecture of the course on a pedestrian historical introduction and then had to scamper through two lectures' worth of material in the last lecture, unable for lack of time to do justice to the most exciting and up-to-date of the topics.

In the absence of any panacea, it is left to the imagination and judgment of teachers to decide in what ways to invest facts with concreteness. These are not problems with unique solutions. The best answers vary between different categories of students, whose particular needs and interests have to be taken into account in planning the teaching approach. But the general requirement is always the same: the teacher has to put facts into contexts such that they become part of intellectual processes other than mere memorization. Success in doing this is the key to good teaching.

The very real difficulty of achieving this kind of success may help to account for the prevalence of the misconception that science equals facts. For the teacher who lacks inspiration or has lost what he once had, the easiest thing is to lapse into mere recital of facts. Thus many people come away with an excessively factual view of science merely because they have been indifferently taught. However unfortunate this may be, it is not really surprising. Inspired teaching is, naturally enough, the exception rather than the rule. Moreover, other subjects are also not immune from the same failing. Even subjects like history and classics, supposedly the stuff of liberal education and stimulants of the mind, can and have been reduced to a dull grind of facts.

The relation of the real thing to the teaching material extracted or derived from it is, however, a peculiar or even unique one in the case of science. It is so very easy to lose the elements of concreteness in going from science as practised to science as taught. What is left is just the facts and theories, because these are the facets of science that are easiest to write down in textbooks and to teach. Of course, it would be entirely impossible— even if it were desirable, which it is not—to teach any branch of science complete with all its details in any conceivable course of practicable length. There is bound to be some 'transmission loss'. The important point is not that some details must be left out, but that some *kinds* of details get left out much more easily than others. The transmission loss is selective, and the bias of the selectivity helps to account for the distortion that the educational process almost inevitably introduces into the picture of science that is handed on to students (section 2b).

To be fair, the blame cannot be laid entirely on teachers and textbook-writers. The difficulties of setting and marking

The Teaching of Science

examinations are a powerful contributory factor. The easiest type of examination question to set and to mark is that which tests pure factual recall; more effort and ingenuity are usually required to devise and operate satisfactory tests of understanding and of the ability to handle information. Where the examinations are public ones with large numbers of candidates, the difficulties may be specially formidable. So it is not only because of its teachability but also because of its examinability that description of nature tends to be disproportionately emphasized at the expense of other facets of science.

c. CREATIVITY IN SCIENCE

In talking about the relation between what happens in education and what happens in the advance of the frontiers of science, it would clearly be good to know in more detail how 'real' science actually does advance. In particular, one would like to know in what ways the mental processes in creative science resemble any that education can generate or stimulate.

Creativity is obviously an absorbing subject, and it is a pity that there is so little that can be said about it that is both firmly based and illuminating. More than one academic discipline might conceivably throw light on this area. Psychologists, for instance, have interested themselves in it and made attempts to describe and assess the factors involved[21]. At present, however, it seems as though the best source of insight is the more reflective and analytical kind of history of science. I think it worth mentioning two authors here—Kuhn and Koestler.

Kuhn[22], in an essay which has attracted quite wide attention, suggests an analysis of science into revolutionary 'paradigm' breaks on the one hand, and on the other the periods of 'normal' science that follow such crucial, direction-changing events. A scientific revolution, such as the Copernican revolution or the overthrow of the phlogiston theory, sets up a new 'paradigm', a model or example of a type of problem and a general way to tackle that type of problem; the work that follows patterns itself on this in its general aims and in adopting similar sets of assumptions, written and unwritten rules of procedure and so on. Thus the potentialities inherent in a paradigm are exploited by the ensuing normal science.

The Nature of the Scientific Process

Kuhn is at pains to emphasize that solving problems within the framework set by a current paradigm is no mere bread-and-butter activity but can be fascinating, demanding and rewarding. Nevertheless, the great bulk of scientific activity does emerge in a relatively prosaic light from his analysis. This is perhaps not calculated to endear it to everybody, but in itself it is not a serious criticism; the glamour of science is often overestimated.

There is, however, a related point on which the whole treatment is distinctly vulnerable to criticism—namely, the implication that there are two sharply separated groups of scientific activity and two distinct classes of advances, those of great and those of small importance and originality. In fact, it is difficult not to be convinced by direct inspection of science that contributions come in all sizes—that there is actually a continuous size distribution in which really major contributions are very rare and minor ones by far the most frequent, but in which intermediate ones occur with intermediate frequency. The view that there are two distinct groups may be a historian's artifact—a result of the not uncommon habit of concentrating studies on crucial events of outstanding importance, or of the historiographic fact that history is most easily written in terms of such events.

Koestler — extending his usual inventiveness in the use of existing words to the forming of new ones—has coined the term 'bisociation' for the essential act in mental creation[23]. Bisociation is binary association—the bringing together of two things that were previously unrelated. Thus Gutenberg's invention of printing with movable type was based on bringing together the idea of the seal for stamping an impression and the idea of the winepress for exerting powerful steady pressure. Darwin's idea of natural selection as the agent of evolution came from associating the ideas of artificial selection by domestic breeding with Malthusian views on the results of the natural tendencies of populations to increase.

Here, too, there is over-emphasis on major discoveries in the discussion as published, but in this case the same treatment can very easily be applied also to minor ones. Indeed, it provides a basis for some kind of measure of the degree of originality in a particular case. The measure is in terms of the 'distance' apart of the two things associated—their degree of unrelatedness before the event. Moreover, this picture can be combined with much that is valuable in Kuhn's discussion of the important role of modelling in science, with only the proviso that more than one model is used in the creation of a new scientific achievement.

With the kind of picture of science that results, I believe that much can be done to describe and analyze scientific work and progress in reasonably realistic ways. Essentially, according to this picture, the mental act in scientific research consists of taking an element or elements from one earlier piece of scientific work and combining it with an element or elements from another. For instance, it is well known that to take a method or technique that has been developed in one area of science and apply it to another is a staple feature of scientific progress. Here the technique comes from one model, the problem and other details from another. The technique may, of course, take any of a number of forms; it may be a mathematical one, or a practical experimental one, or just a piece of instrumentation. In fact, any one or more of the things I have referred to above as 'facets' of a scientific achievement may be taken from a model and used again in the new context of the current piece of scientific work.

All that this really amounts to saying is that it is usually possible to find historical antecedents for any piece of work. It does not matter, from the present point of view at least, whether the workers in question were or were not conscious of those antecedents; the difference between genuine ignorance and subconscious awareness is often impossible to determine, even by the workers themselves after the event. Nor does it matter if more than two antecedents are recognized; the question whether this means a series of bisociations, or one act of associating more than two things, also turns out often to hang on very fine distinctions indeed.

It is not necessary, either, to embark on a discussion of whether there is such a thing as a totally new idea, an idea of absolute novelty, created *de novo* and not from previous ideas. It is merely specious to deny that new arrangements of existing units do contain genuine novelty; new things can, after all, be built with the pieces in a toy construction set, new symphonies can be written without using notes hitherto unused, the writing of new books does not demand the creation of new words, and new kinds of living organisms have evolved while the number of different kinds of atoms involved has not increased. There is, in any case, a continuous and steady influx of undoubtedly genuine novelty into science in the form of new empirical observations.

If one accepts that there is any degree of validity in analyzing science in these terms, then one has a framework in which to view the acquisition of knowledge in the development of scientists. Education and training must clearly provide for the necessity to build up a stock from which elements can be taken for fruitful bisociations. Such a stock will have to include facts of many kinds — not merely individual empirical facts but also theories, techniques and preferably, indeed, whole scientific situations with much of the elements of 'concreteness' as described earlier (section 2c).

Regarding the best ways of setting about providing for the acquisition of such stocks by budding scientists, there are three points that call for comment. The first concerns the balance between particular facts and general principles. It is clearly not the only or even the main function of education to load up with a ballast of facts that will see the recipient safely through the voyage of a scientific career. Rather, the purpose should be to provide the basis and the skills to continue to absorb and use relevant information. But this cannot be done in the absence of facts. Skill in handling facts—possibly the chief and overriding purpose of good education—cannot be developed without a great deal of working on facts. Practice has to be got in mastering them, absorbing them, arranging them, restating them, developing them into themes and deploying them for arguments.

It is because of this that it is dangerous to accept too readily that courses should provide 'principles, not facts' (cf. section 4d). Principles may be admirable aids in handling facts, but by themselves they may be too abstract. A policy of 'principles only' may fail to achieve any degree of the concreteness that brings science to life. The vast bulk of scientific activity deals not with disembodied principles but with particular facts about the physical world, related as closely as possible to any theory that may be available. Moreover, although everyone agrees that 'mere facts' can be learned after the end of formal education, it seems sometimes to be assumed that the mastering of principles must end abruptly with graduation. There is no good justification for this assumption if the mind-training function is properly carried out; and there should therefore be no need to become panic-stricken if a first degree course does not cover all the theory (see the more extended discussion of first degree standards in section 4f, and also section 5j). The price of such panic is haste in screwing up the level of conceptual and theoretical sophistication, at the expense of considering particular cases, the information in which may admittedly be more or less trivial in itself but which is justified by the effect it has in illustrating the theory and giving it body. There may be exceptions—the occasional outstandingly gifted theoretician springs to mind—but in most cases the likely result is more haste, less speed. Good teaching, maintaining a judicious balance between particular facts and general principles, may be jeopardized just as much by syllabuses that are over-ambitious on theory as by those that are cluttered by empirical facts.

The second point follows naturally and inevitably from the first. Institutionally as well as pedagogically, in the organization and the regulations of teaching bodies as well as in the planning of the teaching approach, it should be clearly recognized that education need not end with any certificate, diploma, degree or doctorate. The British educational system could probably with advantage go further than it does at present to open its doors and extend a welcome to those who wish to continue their education by short courses or to work part-time for higher qualifications, not excluding research degrees.

Thirdly, the question is raised of the optimum range over which a stock of knowledge should be built up. The study in depth on which so much reliance is placed in English education is usually taken to mean concentration on a relatively narrow range. It is true that this policy is relatively safe. A student who has learned chemical techniques is highly likely to be able to apply them successfully to new chemical compounds. It is much less likely that study in two apparently unrelated fields will pay off in either—that, for instance, anything in a knowledge of plasma physics could be applied successfully to population genetics, or *vice versa*. If, however, some such unlikely bisociation worked, it would be highly original. As I have mentioned above, the further apart the two things bisociated were before the event, the greater is the degree of originality in bisociating them. The less related they seemed initially, the greater is the

The Nature of the Scientific Process

achievement of relating them. Thus one has—as so often—an inverse relation between the probability of success and the value of that success if achieved; one has to strike a balance between playing for a safe small prize or trying a long shot for a big one.

Considerations along these lines—the hope of increasing the chances of finding new connections—are sometimes used to press for breadth in education. In fact, though, they probably argue more for multiple specialization (section 5i) than for thinly spread breadth (see, however, section 4e for the pitfalls that lurk around the concepts of breadth and depth in education). What they point to as desirable is not so much scratching at a large surface as 'sinking boreholes' in knowledge at moderate spacings in the hope of some possibly unexpected but fruitful meeting.

f. INTERNAL AND EXTERNAL FACTORS

If one asks what, in broad terms, are the influences which affect the general direction of scientific advance — leaving aside, of course, the details of local and temporary incidents and accidents —one can distinguish two main types of possibilities, the internalist and the externalist. According to the internalist view, science is an essentially autonomous activity whose development is governed essentially by intrinsic factors—its inner logic and impetus and the inter-relations among its branches. It does, of course, have effects outside itself, applications and implications desirable and undesirable; but these are extraneous to the mainstream of science, incidental side-effects which exert no major influence on the development of the activity of which they are the fruits.

One expression of this type of view is what might be called the 'biological organism' model of science. The implication in likening science to a living thing is that its growth normally takes place in a 'balanced' way and that it might be unhealthy to interfere from outside, suppressing one branch or unduly forcing another. This notion of balance has about it something of a mystic quality. It suggests that somehow, apart from artificial perturbations that may be allowed to interfere, science arrives by itself at the right distribution of effort between different sectors—the right ratios between, say, high energy nuclear physics, radio-astronomy, heterocyclic chemistry, bacterial genetics and marine ecology. Any confidence that this is really so is hard to justify. The actual balance in any country or in the world as a whole is just the sum total of what scientists in fact happen to be doing. It is very much open to doubt whether there is necessarily any approximation to 'rightness' about it, or even whether there is a satisfactory standard by which one could judge what the 'right' balance is.

Nevertheless, the arguments for leaving science to grow freely and unchecked cannot be dismissed out of hand. One of the most powerful short statements is to be found in Polanyi's article *The Republic of Science*[24]. Polanyi maintains, in effect, that only by allowing the individual initiatives of scientists free play can we be sure of optimizing the use of scientific resources. The argument proceeds by analogy with economic liberalism. There is a sort of market mechanism, something like Adam Smith's 'invisible hand', which directs efforts into those areas where work is likely to have the highest scientific value. This co-ordination is achieved by the way in which each individual adjusts his own efforts to the results obtained by others. Attempts to organize science under any central authority would in fact paralyze this co-operation of individual efforts and reduce its effectiveness to that of the single central authority. Moreover, the ambition to guide science into socially beneficent channels, however generous the sentiments from which it springs, is impossible to achieve, for science 'can advance only by essentially unpredictable steps, pursuing problems of its own, and the practical benefits of these advances will be incidental and hence doubly unpredictable'. Thus 'any attempt at guiding scientific research towards a purpose other than its own is an attempt to deflect it from the advancement of science'. It follows that the allocation of money to science should be guided by the advice of scientific and not of other opinion, and 'adulteration' of science by political, commercial or other outside interests is to be avoided.

All this need not, however, be taken to suggest that science operates in a social vacuum. In actual fact, it obviously does not; it does not stand outside that 'total interconnectedness' on which students of society insist. Some of the ways in which society acts on science are obvious enough. There are direct prohibition and regulated control, as of the vivisection of human beings and

The Nature of the Scientific Process

animals respectively; there are limitations on money and on manpower, normally operative right across the board, though with very variable stringency; most obvious of all, sometimes brutally so, there is the way branches of science get caught up in commercial or military interests and become correspondingly infused with resources and infected with goal-consciousness.

Quite apart from the power of the blunderbuss and the pursestring, there are also more subtle ways in which external influences are brought to bear on science. Despite the comicstrip picture of absent-minded professors absorbed in their science and totally oblivious of all else, scientists are not in general totally unaware of the environment in which they live. To suppose that they are is what Needham[25] has called a 'Manichaean heresy' — it seems to deny that scientists have bodies and live social lives and are therefore subject to influences from outside. The effect on scientists of pressures and needs in the social *milieu* in which they live is often underestimated, partly because scientists themselves may not be fully aware of it. Since it acts by conditioning scientists' own choices, it can operate without necessarily restricting their individual and corporate freedom in the exercise of their profession. Scientists may feel themselves to stand in splendid isolation when in fact a variety of factors external to science has played a part in moulding their interests and values. The autonomy of science, in short, may be partly illusory.

There is a good illustration of this in a paper by Merton[26] which has become something of a classic. Although it is based on historical material from the seventeenth century, it deals with principles of general applicability and is often quoted in modern discussions. Taking a sociologist's look at the history of science, Merton studied the topics chosen by scientists in seventeenth century England by analysing the minutes of the newly founded Royal Society for the years 1661, 1662, 1686 and 1687. Well over half of the researches discussed at meetings during these years, he found, were related directly or indirectly to socioeconomic needs, principally in the fields of marine transport, mining and military problems.

The interpretation of these facts is of more than purely historical interest. While there is no need to lapse into the 'vulgar materialism' of supposing that socio-economic factors account

The Teaching of Science

exhaustively for the whole complex of scientific activity, it is quite clear that the dominant themes of science in seventeenth century England were determined to an appreciable extent by the social conditions of the time. Merton argues that it would be a mistake to suppose that the only channel for this influence was the deliberately utilitarian motivation of some scientists. There is also a less direct relationship between science and social needs in that 'certain problems and materials for their solution come to the attention of scientists although they need not be cognizant of the practical exigencies from which they derive'. Indeed, analysing motives may give a quite misleading picture of the modes by which socio-economic factors exert influences on science. The motives of scientists may range from personal ambition to a wholly disinterested desire to know, but that does not alter the demonstrable fact that the subjects that seventeenth century scientists chose to work on were largely in areas which seemed relevant to the major practical problems of the time. Merton concludes that it can be said, with suitable provisos, that 'necessity is the (foster) mother of invention and the grandparent of scientific advance'.

No special perspicacity is needed to see that it is still true today that necessity is at least one of the grandparents of scientific advance, even though marine transport and mining no longer rank with military requirements among the three main sources of necessity. It is still true, too, that the grandparental influence is not totally overt and is not exhaustively measured by the number of scientists who are avowedly 'applied'. Among the attitudes of university scientists in Britain to the question of the applicability of their work for useful purposes, one can detect some curious strains which are not always free of self-deception at best and hypocrisy at worst. Protestations of 'purity' are still common. 'I am pure, thou art applied, he is technological'—that is still the largely accepted grammar of scientific snobbery. Yet one gets the impression all the same that there are few who would not be tickled pink if their work did turn out to have practical usefulness, even if they would not wish to stoop deliberately to seek it.

Often academic scientists are good at thinking of areas of potential practical relevance of their work when it comes to applying for financial support from outside bodies; and it is not

The Nature of the Scientific Process

unknown for the areas to be specified differently for the benefit of different grant-giving bodies. Rightly or wrongly, this seems not to be considered dishonest, and the exercise may be a genuinely useful one in that it at least makes scientists think about various possible applications of their work. There is a valid argument here for encouraging multiple channels of external funding for university research, and for not making it too easy for scientists to get their grants. Some degree of tightness encourages a certain amount of what Flowers[27] has called 'anisotropy' in the development of science. The purely academic tendency is for isotropic growth, in which all lines of development from a given discovery are regarded as equally acceptable. A certain loading of the dice in favour of lines that look like turning out to be socially or economically valuable is not necessarily unhealthy.

In ways such as these, external influences do filter in on science even in its remote academic fastnesses. Nevertheless, the feeling has been growing in Britain quite markedly in recent years that the interaction between science and society is not effective enough, and that science has remained too insensitive to social and economic needs. Public concern has developed because the increase in the scale of the resources devoted to science has reached a level at which it is quite big enough to be noticed in terms of national accounting. Indeed, the rate of growth recently has been such as to make the matter seem urgent. The total amount that was spent on scientific and technological research in the United Kingdom in 1964-65 is estimated at £771 million, or 2·7% of the gross national product. Nine years earlier it was about £300 million, accounting for 1·8% of the gross national product. Growth was particularly rapid in the universities and technical colleges, where research expenditure almost quadrupled from £14·4 million to £55·9 million[28].

Clearly, growth rates of anything like these magnitudes cannot be continued indefinitely. The conclusion seems inescapable that it will be necessary in future to exercise greater selectivity in promoting science. As the Council for Scientific Policy recognized in 1966, the question at issue is only 'when, and at what rate, and on what criteria, the levelling-off of the growth rate should take place'[29]. Undoubtedly this will demand changes in attitudes and in the scientific environment that will not be achieved painlessly, but society as a whole need not, perhaps, take too alarmist a view of the prospects. Inability (or unwillingness) indefinitely to sustain free growth is not necessarily a catastrophic failure to provide for something essential to future vigour and prosperity (section 3g). One is tempted to give the 'biological organism' model a twist and point out that pruning has the intention and the effect of removing dead wood so as to encourage the growth of new and vigorous shoots. In so far as pruning is also a means of shaping, it may be a healthy mechanism for helping to adjust science to the environment in which it operates.

The financial problem is not the only or even the major one. In discussing the shares of scarce resources that go into science as a whole and into different areas of it, attention should be focused at least as much on manpower as on money, and especially on the most able and highly qualified manpower. In Britain, the best brains tend to prefer sectors of science relatively insulated from social and economic needs. The attractiveness to scientists of the higher education system, at the expense of industry, has been causing concern, especially since it affects particularly those with honours degrees of high class and/or higher degrees. The Interim Swann Report concluded in 1966 that 'the trend away from industry is most marked in those with the highest academic attainments'[30]. The corresponding phenomenon at the earlier stage of the transition from school to university is quite familiar to those concerned with applications and admissions to universities. Minimum entry standards in many applied science departments are lower than is usual in the major pure science subjects. Among university admissions officers, there is a continuing series of jokes about headmasters who, commenting on candidates for university entrance, deliver themselves to the effect that 'Smith lacks the intellectual calibre for pure science but should do well at something more applied'. Needless to say, the more applied the university department, the sicker the jokes.

To some extent, the obtaining system of preferences is at least easy to explain. One might expect *a priori* that the educational system should have a built-in tendency to favour internalist motivation. Students at university, as well as pupils at school, tend to identify with their teachers; the better they are at their studies, the more likely they are to take on the values of the environment in which they are being educated. The situation is not helped by the fact that relatively few teachers have the kind of experience that gives real sympathy with science outside the educational system. For a number of reasons (the financial one not least among them), those most successful in industrial or other applied research are least likely, in general, to find their ways into teaching jobs. Thus distrust of applied science as an activity worth the attention of good brains is added to the general disdain of anything that smacks of commerciality which infects in particular the élite educational institutions of Britain.

The real basis for the preference of many of the ablest scientists for the purest science is, of course, to be found more in social convention than in intrinsic features of the subjects. The nature of the process by which applied science operates is in many respects similar to that of pure science. Similar types of facets go to make up new achievements; the intellectual demands are comparable and so are the ingenuity and creativity required to forge the way ahead. The main differences lie in the criteria of desirability of the solutions aimed at, not in the manner of achieving them. A look beyond our own shores serves to show the arbitrariness of the British system of preferences. Other countries order their priorities differently. In Japan, we are told, 'the very brightest boys go into engineering, 30 per cent of top management are engineers, and all the girls want to marry one'[31].

So the pressure is on in Britain to tighten the coupling between the activities of scientists and the needs of society. Accusing fingers are pointed at the disparity between the high standard of British pure science and the failure to achieve hoped-for increases in national prosperity. Nobel prizes come flooding in—there were 20 British prizewinners in science between 1950 and 1967 —but the scientific miracles have not been accompanied by economic ones. How, it is being asked, can we more effectively harness science as a force for the general good? How can we minimize the extent to which it merely free-wheels along independently of the other activities and aspirations of society, parasitic on them or even actively anti-social? In what ways should we and could we make scientists more aware of society and society of science?

Before we can even begin to answer these momentous questions, we must take a look at the different ways in which science carries social implications and exerts social effects. This is what the next chapter sets out to do.

CHAPTER THREE

THE SOCIAL IMPLICATIONS OF SCIENCE

a. THE FUNDAMENTAL POLARITY

Scientists do science for mixtures of any or all of the usual variety of reasons—for fun, for kicks, out of idealism or sheer curiosity, because they can't think of anything better, to earn money to support their families, to get a feeling of power, to prove themselves, to impress their friends, to win fame and public esteem. This range of motivational factors is not very different from those which drive other people to engage in a wide variety of other activities. There are, surely, callings where self-sacrificing devotion to the public good plays on average a greater role. Why, then, should society not only allow scientists to practise their craft but also support them—as it does, by and large—on a massive scale?

There are many different kinds of science and therefore many different types of justification. Underlying them, however, are two major kinds of consideration, two kinds of goal which exercise pulls on scientific endeavour. Though not exactly opposites, these two often appear to pull in different directions. They are, in a way, like two poles of attraction which set up a field of force within which views on the social repercussions of science fall and in terms of which particular cases can be analyzed. The extremes which set up this fundamental polarity adopt primarily intellectual and materialist criteria respectively. Simply—and therefore roughly—they can be described as follows. The one regards science as one of the greatest adventures of the human mind—possibly the greatest it has ever undertaken. The other sees in science the principal agent we have at our disposal for taming and transforming our material environment and providing wealth and welfare for ourselves.

The Teaching of Science

Put simply like this in terms of its bare bones, the matter may sound like a straightforward antithesis. In fact, however, it is by no means simple. The two poles do not merely pull against each other—the relationship between them is a lot more complicated than simple opposition; they interact in ways which are sometimes far from obvious on the surface and which may be difficult in the extreme to disentangle. Accordingly, they deserve more than cursory scrutiny here.

It is as well to insist, in the first place, that both have their own idealism (not 'idealism' in the technical philosophical sense of the word, of course, but in the everyday sense of motivation by ideals that are humanitarian and philanthropic). The dichotomy is *not* between the 'pure', noble and disinterested search for knowledge on the one hand and the pursuit of base self-interest on the other. To conquer poverty and famine and disease, to put cheap power at everybody's fingertips, to provide machines to take the sweat and the chores out of life—these are things which are obviously in the interests of communities, not just of the individuals who undertake them; they solve other people's problems and help to improve the quality of life for many people who have nothing at all to do with developing or implementing the innovations concerned. Undoubtedly it is true that the sort of work that has these effects often gets entangled with the profit motive; but anyone who is prepared to recognize that this can work for as well as against the public interest—and that leaves enough latitude to accommodate a very wide range of opinion indeed between the two political extremes—will agree that an activity does not necessarily become anti-social just because profit is made from it.

Conversely, just as science for wealth is not always and totally base, so science for knowledge is not always and totally noble. The detachment of the pure scientist from practical issues may spring not only from disinterested selflessness but also from less admirable causes, such as the wish to be free to do what he likes without submitting to the discipline of external pressures, or a certain kind of narrow-mindedness which makes him unwilling to extend his intellectual horizons beyond the academic scene, or a lack of courage to face the hurly-burly of life outside the groves of Academe.

So one cannot separate the two main aims of science just by

the criterion of the nobility of the motivation. Merely to resolve to adopt a high-minded attitude to science does not take one far, because there is no single high-minded attitude to adopt.

A second point on which it is important to insist is that both the main functions of science are—or at least can be—genuinely *social* ones. To regard the pursuit of scientific knowledge irrespective of applications as being only for the intellectual satisfaction of scientists is not just an oversimplification but a serious error of categorization. Potentially at least, the lay public can get some of the benefit of 'science as culture'—of its knowledge and its ways of thought and even of methodological fall-out or spin-off from it. The community can be enriched by it, just as it can be enriched by scholarship in general or by the cultivation of the fine arts; though the precise ways in which this enrichment takes place will need to be looked into more closely by and by (see sections 3d and 3e). Conversely, it is equally true that scientists can share, both as individuals and corporately as a profession, in any additional wealth that the community can create.

Looked at from an *a priori* philosophical starting point, it is perhaps not surprising that the discussion of the aims and ideals of science never seems to be able to get far away from the internal strains and stresses set up by conflict between intellectual and materialist goals. Natural science operates, so to speak, across the interface between the realms of mind and matter. Because the essence of the whole enterprise consists precisely in acting across this interface, it is inevitable that the two sides should have something approaching parity of status and esteem—more so than in other activities, where the balance is often less even. In the literary arts, for instance, the material manifestations are quite clearly no more than incidental. (No offence to the bibliomanes, but for most readers of Shakespeare the play's the thing.) To some extent, the same is true even of the visual arts—they have to have material embodiment but there can be no doubt which is the means and which the end. The converse situation obtains in technology. Here brainpower is a means which helps to achieve material ends; however great the demands made on it, its role is clearly that of a tool. In science, however, it is the interplay between theory and empirical fact that is central. The reasoning and speculation of even the most theoretical of

The Teaching of Science

physicists must have to do in a crucial sense with the results of possible experiments, otherwise it is not part of natural science; neither is any event in the material world a part of science unless it is intellectually processed in some way.

This way of viewing the matter is based, admittedly, on a straightforward and rather unsophisticated Cartesian dualism between mind and matter, and it is not hard to see ways in which it is an oversimplification. Computer hardware can solve abstract mathematical problems; technology has its aesthetics as well as its own *sui generis* effect on knowledge. (It has been plausibly argued that early nineteenth century science owed more to the steam engine than the steam engine to science, and parallel situations exist today.) Nevertheless, there does seem to be some virtue in this simple way of looking at the situation and formulating its essentials.

Such philosophical generalities are not, however, the most satisfying way to illuminate an issue for most people. Genuine clarification is often to be found in the concrete realities of history rather than in the abstract analyses of philosophy. Historical perspectives and parallels and examination of past failures and successes often help people to see beyond the surface of issues and to glimpse something of the implications, ramifications and limitations involved. The drawing of object-lessons out of history is, it is true, a game which is academically suspect and possibly dangerous in practice—historical parallels, like the geometrical kind, never meet in identity; but in favourable cases the leading features do emerge more clearly and better defined in their relatively undeveloped beginnings. It seems worth while, therefore, to make a historical digression here to consider the social implications of science in the actual settings of historical situations.

That key period in the origin of modern science, the scientific revolution of the sixteenth and seventeenth centuries, once again turns out to be particularly instructive. It has been much studied (as quantity of study goes in the history of science) for the light it throws on the nature of scientific thought and the ways in which science advances; but it seems as yet to be less widely appreciated that one can also see here the origins of the two principal currents by which science has made an impact on society. With just a little simplification, just a modicum of licence in historical interpretation, one can see them exemplified—made

The Social Implications of Science

incarnate, so to speak—in the persons of two men who both flourished in the early part of the seventeenth century, Galileo Galilei and Francis Bacon respectively. The nature of their contributions is well known; in what follows, I will try to assess the significance of what they did from the standpoint not so much of science itself as of the science-society relationship.

b. GALILEO'S CAMPAIGN OF CULTURAL PROPAGANDA

Galileo stands here principally for the wider intellectual and cultural value of science. This must certainly not be taken to mean, however, that he despised practical applications. In his great book on mechanics, the *Discourses on Two New Sciences*, he commented on the intellectual stimulus to be got from watching the instruments and machines in use at the Venetian arsenal. When applying for a post that would take him back home from Padua to Florence—in 1610, soon after his first great discoveries with the telescope—he was not above mentioning the value of his mathematical mechanics for 'the practice of fortification, ordnance, assaults, sieges, estimation of distances, artillery matters, the uses of various instruments, and so on'[1]. On paper at least he was quite prepared to apply scientific knowledge to the practical problems of his day.

But it is principally for his struggle to win acceptance for Copernicanism that he has gone down in history. Koestler[2] has it that he was actually driven largely by selfishness and arrogance, and there may well be a good deal of justification for these charges, but they are beside the point here because they do not alter the fact that he marked a real turning point in cultural history. Thus, as Geymonat emphasizes in his interesting book[3], Galileo seems to have been guided by a faith that human reason can, by scientific research, 'clear up the most deceitful misunderstandings, overcome all ancient prejudices, strip from nature every secret'—that it is 'the spur that drives every man to love truth and feel joy when he succeeds in freeing himself from error'.

Moreover, 'science is not a matter of restricting the liberating function of reason to some specialists, but of projecting it to all men in order to awaken them, stimulate them, render them ever more conscious'. It was with this kind of conviction in mind,

The Teaching of Science

Geymonat argues, that he embarked on his campaign of 'cultural propaganda' to spread belief in Copernicanism (or rather, in its basic tenet, heliocentrism) to the greatest possible number of people. He saw in this the key to establishing the spirit of the new science on a wide basis in society. The significance of the fact that he wrote some of his major works in Italian rather than Latin then becomes understandable; it was an attempt to reach an audience beyond the world of scholarship. Not that he exactly 'brought astronomy to the market-places', as Brecht suggests in his play on the subject[4], but at least he could address himself to thoughtful people outside the universities and the church.

Similarly, Popper[5] regards the 'Galilean' conception of science as one that gives it genuine and great intellectual power. Contrary to those humbler modern views which, basing themselves on positivist doctrines, see science as merely a means of predicting phenomena, this one insists that it can and does reveal to us new worlds that were previously hidden. It does not merely provide rules for us to predict events and calculate how they will happen, it also opens up to us the worlds of galaxies and sub-atomic particles and the inner mechanisms of living bodies. Thus it is not just 'glorified plumbing' but the latest phase in the triumph of the human mind, the rightful heir and worthy modern representative of the tradition of rational and critical discussion derived from the Greeks.

There is a very substantial and significant element of truth in all this. Galileo's achievement was in one way every bit as great as his admirers insist. But it was not quite as one-sided as the impressions of it that are widely current, and this aspect of it also has its significance.

Galileo was in effect asking the western world to change its view of the universe because he had seen through his telescope that Jupiter has moons revolving round it and that Venus shows phases rather like those of the moon. This amounted in practice to more than just settling the question of whether the sun moves round the earth or the earth round the sun. The issue at stake was man's place in the universe—not just in the sense of his physical location in it but in the sense of the meaning of his existence. The old geocentric cosmology was more than a scheme in which known astronomical and physical facts interlocked in intimate and not too unsatisfactory ways. In its mediaeval versions, it had become also a sort of ethical allegory, in which man's relation to good and evil was symbolized by his position between the immutable perfection of the heavens above and the depths of hell down below in the centre of the earth.

This comprehensive world-view was now to be overturned because of astronomical evidence which was really rather flimsy, at least to the extent that Galileo himself used it. Had he been able to produce convincing proof, the outcome might have been happier for all concerned. Cardinal Bellarmine recorded his willingness to accept physical proof in a letter written in 1615, the year before the first of the two crises between Galileo and the church blew up. 'I say that if there were a true demonstration that the sun was in the centre of the universe ... then it would be necessary to use careful consideration in explaining the Scriptures that seemed contrary, and we should rather have to say that we do not understand them than to say that something is false which had been proven. But I do not think there is any such demonstration, since none has been shown to me.'[6]

Reflecting on this situation helps to bring home to one the wider implications of two points about science that have already been touched on (section 2b). There can be no question, on the one hand, about the fact that science does not operate solely and exclusively by infallible reason; and, on the other hand, the question remains wide open of where the boundaries of science are set—of how far across the spectrum of human interests science and its methods are applicable and relevant.

The grounds on which reason is sometimes seen as the road to salvation for humanity are not easy to pin down, but the main factor seems to be the property that its conclusions have of commanding universal assent. Normal people everywhere readily agree to logical inferences. It has required no bitter strife in history to establish that two plus two equals four; no great issues raised by this have led to political battles or persecutions, and no great wars have been sparked off by it. But an age of science is not just an age of sweet reason. How could it be, when science itself depends also on non-rational processes? It is really rather naïve to suppose that the triumph of science will—or ever could —bathe everything in the warm and peaceful glow of rationality.

Science has, in any case, no monopoly of rationality. Quite on the contrary—the mediaeval tradition of scholasticism which

Galileo helped to undermine was in some ways more rational, in that it relied more exclusively on the reasoning faculty of the human mind. Its main weakness lay in the scant attention it paid to sense experience, the evidence of empirical observations; and an important ingredient of Galileo's achievement concerned precisely this point—he helped to establish sense experience as a secure source of knowledge, an authority co-equal with reason.

It is the dual primacy of rationality and empiricism that forms the Achilles' heel of science. Fallibility arises from the way in which the demands of these twin arbiters of truth are combined to go beyond where either alone can lead. There is serious doubt among philosophers whether the formation of general theories from particular facts can be a purely rational or logical process; it seems that it can only be done with some admixture of guesswork or inspiration or something that falls short of logic (or transcends it, according to the point of view). The other part of science, as seen in the hypothetico-deductive picture of it (section 2b), is the deduction of particular facts from general theories, and this can, of course, be done purely by logic—it is often done with the aid of mathematics. It is here that strict reasoning plays its role—but only in this phase of the activity, not dominating and pervading the whole of the scientific process.

To these doubts about the absoluteness of the intellectual authority of science must be added doubts about the range over which it extends. On its own chosen ground, the power of science may be so great—despite the qualifications just mentioned—as to brook no interference from outside. Attempts to dictate conclusions about scientific matters on the grounds of ideology of any kind are nowadays regarded as ludicrous by virtually everyone (thank goodness!). There have, it is true, been exceptions to this in recent history; in Nazi Germany, there was the 'Jewish physics' of Einstein as distinct from Aryan physics'[7]; in Russia, progressive Soviet biology has been contrasted with the 'bourgeois' genetics based on the work of Mendel, Morgan and Weismann[8,9]; but such cases have been fortunately few and are now, in general, thoroughly discredited.

The intellectual authority of science does not, however, hold sway universally, however powerful it may be on its native ground. Its conclusions, within the area that is clearly natural science, can properly be attacked and defended only by its own methods and within its own terms of reference. But the applicability and relevance of scientific ways of thought certainly have their boundaries, even though the placing and definition of these boundaries is by no means a simple and straightforward matter. Indeed, as the argument about science in politics (section 2b) shows, the issue is very far from dead.

In Galileo's case, the limits against which science came up were set by theological considerations. The famous letter to the Grand Duchess Christina[10], which contains the fullest discussion Galileo has left of the relation between science and theology, recognizes the place of theology as 'queen of all the sciences' on the grounds that it 'excels in dignity all the subjects which compose the other sciences'. There is no argument against the proposition that its subject-matter is 'more sublime'. Galileo pleads only that this should not entitle it to assume authority in the 'humbler speculation of the subordinate sciences'. 'Why, this would be as if an absolute despot, being neither a physician nor an architect but knowing himself free to command, should undertake to administer medicines and erect buildings according to his whim—at grave peril to his poor patients' lives, and the speedy collapse of his edifices.'

In the twentieth century, it may not be predominantly theology that imposes limits on the jurisdiction of science, but purposes and values still have to be set somehow. Magnificent though the achievements of science are, they remain no more than solutions of limited problems within the great mysteries of existence. It is as such that we must accept them. No doubt they can deeply affect old views on the meaning and the purposes of life; certainly they can be influential in moulding our new ones; but they cannot provide an independent, autonomous and universally acceptable system of values. Science triumphant will not bring this age-old debate to a satisfactory conclusion.

c. BACON'S VISION OF SCIENCE ORGANIZED TO GIVE MASTERY OVER NATURE

Bacon's background was very different from Galileo's and so, accordingly, was the nature of his contribution. Professionally he was primarily a lawyer, and he had a busy and distinguished public career, rising to the position of Lord Chancellor, which he held from 1618-1621. In fact, he was hardly a scientist at all in any proper sense of the word. Rather, he might be called the 'first statesman of science'[11]. As a statesman, he represents society, formulating the needs and desires of humanity. His strength lay in his vision of the possibilities of what science might do for mankind rather than in any great insight into how it might be done, though even on this matter he had some interesting suggestions to make.

Like Galileo, he devoted much of his effort to a propaganda campaign, though in his case the principal target was the support of the English monarchy. Like Galileo, too, he was not really successful in his own lifetime. His grandiose schemes were not implemented, though the foundation of the Royal Society later in the seventeenth century was in some measure a fulfilment of his dreams.

Particular schemes apart, his great contribution was to bring out the great humanitarian idealism that can inform, guide and drive science to meet practical needs. A philanthropist rather than a philosopher, he modestly called himself on one occasion. 'In challenging men with such earnestness to win power over nature in order to improve the conditions of human life he kindled a new conscience in mankind'[12]. His message amounts to this—that for scientists to devote themselves to 'glorified plumbing' is not necessarily a come-down from the sublime to the prosaic. On the contrary, it is in a real sense the public-spirited course to take, since glorified plumbing is, after all, what millions in the world need or want. To ignore this is to leave undone something that ought to be done. The scientist who, guided by idealism of another sort, will not deign to consider practical applications can be charged with indifference to problems that could be within his power to solve—a sin of omission, at least.

A most significant thing about Bacon's contribution is the literary talent he put into proclaiming his message. His prose, at its best, is among the finest that England has produced. The pieces he calls 'aphorisms' are long-winded at times, but when he is genuinely aphoristic he displays a 'wonderful talent for packing thought close and rendering it portable', as Macaulay put it. Few have excelled him in the art of making a few short words pack a real punch. His works are, accordingly, real treasure chests for seekers of apt quotations, and their quality is so undimmed by age that a selection from them could make an admirable vade-mecum for speakers and writers on scientific affairs even today.

In short, then, Bacon's contribution was to show how applied science can be both morally and culturally respectable. He remains a source of inspiration to all those who see in science not only an intellectual game but also a force to be harnessed so as to master nature for the benefit of mankind.

The main lines of his campaign, later developed at great length, are summarized in a concise and convenient form in a piece called *In Praise of Knowledge*[13], which was written in 1592, when he was still quite a young man of 31. The pleasures of the intellect, he says in this short piece, are the greatest of all pleasures—but he goes on immediately to ask, are they to be 'only of delight, and not of discovery?' And so he very soon poses the momentous question: 'is truth barren?' Just three short words, but they are pregnant with significance. Is knowledge to be only for its own sake, or can we use it as a help in doing things? 'Shall we not thereby be able to produce worthy effects, and to endow the life of man with infinite commodities?'

In the way Bacon goes on to condemn the kinds of learning current in his day, one can sense an undercurrent of moral indignation. They seem *wrong*—not necessarily and not only in the sense of being false but above all in the sense of being misdirected. 'Are we the richer by one poor invention, by reason of all the learning that hath been this many hundred years?' 'All this is but a web of the wit, it can work nothing.' On the one hand, there is the academic philosophy of the universities, which consists of mere disputations about words; on the other hand, there is the alchemical tradition, which has at least some genuine contact with the physical world through experiment but is ruined nevertheless by the impostures that are rife in it and the obscurity in which its procedures are wrapped. 'The one never faileth to multiply words, and the other ever faileth to multiply gold.'

This futile ineffectiveness Bacon contrasts with the enormous impact made by three inventions of the late middle ages—printing, the use of gunpowder in firearms and the magnetic compass. Revolutions have been wrought by these in learning, in war and in navigation respectively. Yet they were 'but stumbled upon, and lighted on by chance'. How much more might not be achieved by a conscious and planned effort to generate more inventions! It would be quite possible, if only the world of learning could establish a 'happy match between the mind of man and the nature of things'. Through that kind of study, mankind could establish a genuine command over nature. 'The sovereignty of man lieth hid in knowledge.'

Throughout his later life, Bacon strove to find ways of giving fuller and more effective expression in words to the ideals of this early vision. His most specific suggestions for an organization designed to achieve them did not appear until 1627, the year after his death, when *New Atlantis*[14] was printed. In this unfinished work he gave us, within the framework of a utopian fable about a south sea island, his picture of a gentle, dignified dream-world society thoroughly permeated by science. One of the foremost institutions in this society was Salomon's House. Essentially a scientific foundation, a research institute in prototype, it is notable for two things—its scale and its organization. The scale was relatively monumental; to match the monumental aim of 'enlarging the bounds of human empire, to the effecting of all things possible', Bacon's imagination equipped it lavishly with all the facilities he could think of that might conceivably help. The organization was well defined and reflected clearly the need for division of labour and allocation of tasks. There was no question of just leaving science to a few individuals of genius to go in whatever direction their fancy dictated.

Salomon's House had 36 fellows, divided into nine categories. The largest was composed of 12 fellows called Merchants of Light; these sailed to foreign countries to report on the work going on there. In modern terms, their function was what might be called industrial espionage at worst or—in a more favourable light—an attempt to avoid wasteful reduplication of research. The importance attached to them shows appreciation of the fact that, for those who are concerned to turn knowledge to use, rather than to feed the vanity of scientists with the prestige that comes from conceptual originality, discoveries made abroad are just as good as those made at home (cf. section 3g).

The other eight categories are assigned three fellows each. It is worth noting, from the functions they are given, how broadly both the inputs and the outputs of the research process are conceived. Very far indeed from any idea of science as pure thought, there is a close relation to practice in two ways—not only as a desired end-product but also as a potential source of facts about what things there are in the physical world and how they behave in technical processes. There is a large fund of empirical and experimental observations here, ready made if not deliberately planned. Thus, on the 'information service' side, besides a category for searching printed matter, there is one to 'collect the experiments of all mechanical arts' (an 'art' here clearly being what is done by an artisan, not what is done by an artist). Then there is one category for doing experiments, one for correlating the results, and then—most important—a group of three fellows that 'cast about how to draw out . . . things of use and practice for man's life and knowledge . . . these we call dowry-men or Benefactors'.

The remaining three categories devote themselves to a second stage or extra layer of the research process. Their tasks are, respectively, to devise new and more penetrating experiments, to carry out these experiments, and, finally, to formulate the most general laws and theories.

The last stage is thus one for theoreticians, and this may prompt a question. Is knowledge, after all, the final goal of the whole enterprise? Are the 'things of use and practice' just helps and by-products on the way to this goal? As far as Bacon himself is concerned, the answer must be no. He shows merely that he properly values a deeper understanding of nature, recognizing that progress will come not only by improving and refining existing processes but also, and more importantly, by the introduction of entirely new principles. 'Human knowledge and human power meet in one; for where the cause is not known, the effect cannot be produced. Nature to be commanded must be obeyed.'[15] Bacon himself made the celebrated distinction between 'experiments of light' and 'experiments of fruit'[16]. However much he may on occasion extol light, the overall conclusion from the general tenor of his works must be that light is for the sake of fruit, not fruit for the sake of light.

A moment's reflection is enough to show that this is really just what might be expected of a statesman voicing the desires of society at large. Despite all that can be said about its cultural value, most people will look to science for the 'things of use and practice' that come from it. So, in this respect, Bacon runs quite true to type as a non-scientist, an outsider, a layman looking at science from the exterior.

Not only in this respect, furthermore, but also in some others; there are parts of his writings where his amateur status shows through unmistakably. He betrays, in fact, some considerable naïvety regarding science itself. Within the boundaries of science, he is really no more than a tenderfoot.

As illustrative of the limitations of the outsider's approach in general, this is worth enlarging on here. It shows itself on two fronts. The views he expressed on the detailed mechanism of scientific method are not fully realistic, and are overlaid with some degree of self-deception; and his judgments on the validity of conclusions and on the feasibility of objectives are hardly the most perspicacious.

For centuries, Bacon was regarded on the strength of his own word as the apostle of a new science based on inductive method. Many books, even modern ones, accept the substance of this claim, adding merely some sort of apology for the fact that nobody seems to have quite managed to make the method work. All this seems rather odd when one considers in detail what he actually wrote on the subject.

The relevant work is the *Novum Organum*. All through Book I he has many stirring things to say on the need to clear our minds of prejudices and preconceptions and to start afresh on a basis of facts. His emphasis on gathering facts without bias does, it is true, give an impression of inductivism when viewed from a distance and in not too much detail. But when he actually tries to use the method in Book II—the one time he actually makes an attempt to demonstrate it in action—the result is something of an anti-climax.

The occasion is his famous investigation of the nature of heat[17]. His eventual conclusion—that heat is 'a motion of the smaller particles of bodies' — has a quite startling correctness about it, but it is really largely the result of luck and is impressive mainly as a coincidence. Having collected a good number of facts (both real and imaginary) about heat and tabulated them, he seems at last to be on the point of actually performing the long-promised 'true induction'. And then what does he do?

Lamely he apologizes for the fact that he cannot, after all, use true induction because he has not got *all* the facts at his disposal; craves an 'indulgence of the understanding'; and proceeds to set up and knock down one hypothesis after another. At the fifteenth attempt, he at last has a hypothesis which he cannot knock down and which therefore satisfies him. In short, what he has really produced is a glaring example of hypothetico-deductive procedure (section 2b).

It seems an amazing sort of conjurer's trick to play on oneself. And yet one should not, perhaps, blame him too much for having half-deceived himself into a belief in 'true induction'. Plenty of others have, after all, been equally mesmerized by his eloquence, or at least deluded by the same appearances, and they include scientists of great distinction[18].

However, it is also in his assessment of the quality of scientists and the results of their work that he shows his limitations. He mocks Copernicanism, and fails to appreciate Harvey, his contemporary in London. Of Galileo's work, he likes the facile delights of the telescope but not the intellectual rigours of the mathematics. His judgment, in fact, is all too fallible. Everyone is bound to be wrong on some things, but even allowing for this it still remains the case that Bacon can lay claim to no special acuteness of vision in the internal matters of science itself. Those modern authors who read into his works prophecies of most of the particular wonders of modern science and technology are not a little naïve themselves. (Nevertheless, a layman's optimism has some virtue in itself; experts often turn out to be the people who know all the reasons why it is *not* possible to do things.)

Thus Bacon shows both the limitations and the strengths of the outsider's view of science. In stating the needs and wishes that society would like science to meet, the layman may not be in a good position to judge feasibility and he cannot always even formulate problems in realistic ways. Scientific experts may have to reject some requests as quite impossible to meet; others may have to be drastically reformulated before they become practical propositions. Yet the exercise is richly worth while nevertheless. Without it, the experts might never even think of any such projects, but just carry on in their own sweet way, swept along by the self-perpetuating impetus of research. What is called for is a genuine dialogue, with real give and take on both sides,

The Teaching of Science

between those who are in the best position to see the needs and those who can see and assess the technical possibilities for meeting them.

This general type of situation is one that occurs frequently in modern contexts. It applies to the contact between the scientist in a research institute and the social function (industrial or whatever else it may be) that the institute is supposed to serve; or to that between the industrial scientist and the sales force that feeds in information about consumer requirements. In a general way, and on the broadest possible scale, Bacon was the first great spokesman for the various external factors that impose demands or exert pulls on science—he was science's marketing manager, so to speak, or society's scientific liaison officer.

Having now assessed both Galileo's and Bacon's contributions, it is worth remarking that some of the questions of balance that arise from the social implications of science have political overtones. The idea of planning science to meet objectives is naturally likely to be more congenial to those nearer the left end of the political spectrum. A *laissez-faire* approach, merely giving free play to gifted persons, is more like a private enterprise system. More emphasis on setting objectives and organizing teamwork to meet them tends to mean less emphasis on individual (and possibly erratic) genius.

Accordingly, some aspects of Bacon's views on science have proved attractive in recent times to left-wing commentators. He does seem to place his trust in his system rather than in exceptional individuals. The lame man who keeps to the right road, he points out, outstrips the runner who takes a wrong one. He even goes on to claim that 'the course I propose for the discovery of sciences is such as leaves but little to the acuteness and strength of wits, but places all wits and understandings nearly on a level'[19]. Moreover, to the extent that his picture of science is one in which it is driven and guided by economic and social needs rather than by ideas (section 2f), it is bound to attract those with an inclination towards materialism and Marxist economic determinism.

It would be quite absurd to suggest, however, that there is a primarily political issue here. Only the overtones are political, not the fundamentals. Most of the major problems of science policy transcend differences of political ideology. The greatest and most general of such problems, in fact, is quite apolitical; the parties it concerns are not political parties but on the one hand the scientists and on the other the statesmen and all those others who represent social and economic needs. The problem is to generate better understanding between these two groups.

Here, too, there is a moral tale to be drawn from Bacon's life. It is one of failure rather than success, and concerns his relations with Harvey.

I have already mentioned that Bacon failed to appreciate Harvey, despite the fact that he was contemporary with him at the court of James I (indeed, he was attended by him professionally as a physician). But the story does not end there, for Harvey equally failed to appreciate Bacon's vision. He is quoted as having remarked, 'he writes philosophy like a Lord Chancellor'—meaning that he writes about science like a lawyer. The derision of a professional for an amateur is evident. Now Harvey himself was undoubtedly one of the finest scientists of all time; but his mind was preoccupied with matters very different from Bacon's grandiose schemes. A superb observer and experimentalist, he was concerned to clinch his proof of the circulation of the blood, not to build a new and better life for mankind with the aid of science. So these two men, literally crossing each other's paths, each a towering genius in his own way, totally failed to impress each other.

The mutual indifference between Harvey and Bacon shows in prototype the main difficulty of achieving proper contact between scientists and statesmen. Each side needs understanding and appreciation of the other to get the best out of it and to harness it properly, with all that is implied by that for doing good and preventing harm. The fact that the basic motives are not identical does not mean that they cannot, with effort and goodwill on each side, be made compatible.

d. THE CULTURAL VALUE OF SCIENCE

The results of the historical analyses of Galileo's and Bacon's contributions leave us in a better position to discuss the two main currents in the social implications of science and their interrelations in a more modern context. It is convenient again to take the intellectual or cultural one first.

The Teaching of Science

There are, in the first place, two negative points to be made about it. People who look on science as only or primarily an intellectual game sometimes try to justify their positions on the grounds either of escapism or of long-term investment value. Neither of these lines of justification is sound, and it is as well to make this quite clear here.

It is because science clearly has done harm that some people have been tempted to retreat to a purely intellectualistic position. Thus the legendary toast of the Cambridge mathematicians—'here's to pure mathematics, and may it never be of use to anybody!'—is explained by G. H. Hardy's remark: 'this subject has no practical use; that is to say, it cannot be used for promoting directly the destruction of human life or for accentuating the present inequalities in the distribution of wealth'. But this is sheer escapism, for scientists even more obviously than for mathematicians, and it is rightly labelled as such by Bernal[20]. To pretend that one's actions do not have the consequences that they clearly do have is really a not fully adult attitude to take. It reflects a refusal to grow up, a sort of scientist's Peter Pan complex. It is rather like disclaiming responsibility for breaking a window because it was the football and not the foot which hit it.

Escapism will always be with us, but it seems less strong now than it was earlier in the century. This may seem paradoxical in view of the atom bombs of 1945, but a reason can, I think, be found. It has become even more difficult to persuade oneself into the belief that the applications of science can be wished away by a mere effort of will. Science and its effects are now so obviously here to stay that the burying of heads in sand has become more obviously ludicrous than it was.

The best argument in favour of considering science as just an intellectual game without applications or implications is the effect that this could have on some practising scientists. It could, in some cases, deepen their professional commitment and make more single-minded the devotion with which they throw themselves into the task of solving the limited problems they have set themselves. A blinkered horse goes further (to use a metaphor which is not intended to be as unkind as it may sound) because it does not see the distractions on either side of the straight and narrow path.

This does not mean that the distractions are necessarily too

The Social Implications of Science

horrible to contemplate. One is glad to sense that optimism overrides pessimism in the current *Zeitgeist*. Though science is a principal source and agent of change in the modern world, it is not good as a universal scapegoat for all that goes wrong—or at least it seems satisfactory in that role only to those who are not prepared to look deeper[21]. It is not the root of *all* evil. It has the seeds of destruction within itself more obviously than ever; it is continuing to create problems—but it can also help to solve them, and others not of its own making as well. That is why the Baconian inspiration seems fresher than ever today.

This leads on to the second line of false witness on behalf of science as an intellectual game — namely, the idea that to encourage it on that basis is the best way to get an economic return from it in the long run. Confusion often arises here quite unwittingly, for a good deal of self-deception as well as some hypocrisy blurs the line between the idea of science for its own sake and the idea that it will pay off eventually. The real qualitative difference—the difference in kind—is obviously not between short-term and long-term investment but between investing with economic returns in view at any distance and supporting science for its sheer intrinsic intellectual value.

The principle is clear enough. It is applying it that is so difficult. One has to remind oneself of past cases of apparent snow-blindness to applications. In the last century, for instance, radio waves were widely regarded as a discovery for which no major use could be foreseen. So there is always a temptation to agree with Faraday who, when asked what was the use of his work, is said to have replied, 'what is the use of a baby?'[22].

The *cause célèbre* at present is the study of the fundamental particles of matter in high energy nuclear physics. This is of great interest academically—physicists are agreed on that. On the other hand, it is also a very expensive field of research, because enormous accelerators are required to bring particles to high enough energies.

There are no signs of any useful applications emerging from knowledge of these fundamental particles. It is important to be quite clear that this really means exactly what it says: no use can even be envisaged. Perhaps the point can be driven home by a contrast with plasma physics, an area of research which might lead to controlled nuclear fusion and hence to virtually unlimited quantities of energy from water. In this field, the high hopes of the nineteen-fifties have been dashed, and few now believe that the aim will be achieved much before the end of this century, though most believe it will be done next century. A use is clearly there in principle, though it looks like being feasible only in the long run. For the fundamental particle work of high energy nuclear physics, on the other hand, there is not even a potential use in the offing at present.

To justify the enormous budgets that accelerators call for, running in some proposals to hundreds of millions of pounds[23], various arguments are put forward. It is said, for instance, that no really fundamental work in physics has ever failed to find an application in the long run. This may be at least partly a circular argument. If one scoured the nineteenth century literature, one could surely find plenty of work that has found no application. To what extent is it just because of this very fact that it is not regarded as fundamental?

Other arguments are also suspect. That from national economic benefit, for instance, is even weaker. Any nation that opts out now could, in principle at least, buy its way back into the field once its value is proved, if that ever happens. The leaders in a field of research have often not been the main beneficiaries from its applications. Then there are arguments relating to the training and deployment of scientific manpower, where the effects would no doubt be substantial, but also complex and not entirely predictable (section 3g). There is an attractive argument about international collaboration—the sheer scale of the projects forces nations to get together; but there might be ways of getting more international understanding from the same amount of money.

So the only really clear-cut argument in favour of high energy nuclear physics rests on its intellectual value. It is this field of research which gives us what is—in a rather literal sense—our most fundamental knowledge of the physical universe. How highly do we value this as part of human culture? By that, principally, the case must stand or fall[24].

A similar though less clear-cut case is molecular biology, currently the most exciting and glamorous area of the life sciences. Contrary to widespread belief, this has not yet saved many lives or cured many diseases[25]. There are, however, good prospects that it will do so before the end of the century, and it is in this sense that the case is less clear-cut. Nevertheless, these prospects do not obscure the fact that, over and above them, there is a clear and quite independent justification for research in the field. It is giving us what is—again in a rather literal sense—our most fundamental understanding of life. Partially it even qualifies by Pope's criterion, that 'the proper study of mankind is man'.

An analogy may help to clarify the general proposition. There is a very sound economic case for a national investment in art education on the grounds that we need artists to produce designs that will help to sell our engineering products. But obviously there is also a case quite independent of this. Art deserves to be supported for its cultural value—and so does science.

There is an important difference between the two cases, though. It concerns the ways in which the effects are spread through society. How do people other than those actually engaged in the activities come to be affected? Art typically produces something like a painting or a sculpture that people who feel so inclined can go to see. Scientific discoveries, however, are less tangible. The normal form of output for a working scientist is the research paper, for which readership is very limited (section 2a).

It is here that popularization of science comes to be seen in its full significance. All forms of popularization—from books lavishly illustrated with colour plates and glossy monthly magazines to columns in daily newspapers and the occasional few minutes on television or radio—all these can help to maximize the cultural benefits that society gets from science. Popularization is therefore not to be derided. 'Journalism' is a term of abuse in the vocabulary of many academics, and with all too much reason, for newspapers often take more pains over news value than accuracy; but there is such a thing as *la haute vulgarisation* as well as catch-penny journalism[26].

There are other ways that could also be developed for increasing the diffusion of science. Weinberg has suggested, for instance, the possibility of scientific 'fan clubs'[27]. Nevertheless, it clearly remains true that no more than a small minority of the population is ever likely to be reached in an effective way. For 'news from the research front', the audience is likely to remain smaller than that for, say, opera or painting (though possibly not smaller than the *avante-garde* in those fields). The trouble lies, of course, in the high intellectual entrance fee that is imposed by the background of generations of work in accumulating knowledge and screwing up conceptual sophistication. For popularization of types more modest than 'news from the research front', the potential audience is naturally wider. Even so, it still seems to be in a relatively weak position in competing for public interest. An archaeological dig that finds some slight clue to remote antiquity can command front-page space in a 'quality' daily newspaper in a way that a fundamental discovery about the physical universe rarely manages.

Before complaining too bitterly about this, we have to come to grips with a big uncertainty that remains. It is not obvious what *type* of cultural benefit there is that is capable of being shared. Granted that some fair proportion of people not in scientific professions can be reached by science—in what ways are they affected?

One possibility is that science gives a basis for the intercourse of cultivated minds by providing a rich heritage for them to share. As such, it might provide that comfortable, satisfying feeling of harmony with one's fellow-men that comes from having something worth while in common with them. It might provide ingredients for some new kind of intellectuals' *lingua franca*, rather as familiarity with the Greek and Latin literatures (not just the languages) used to do. But if so, is it any more than material for polite dinner-table conversation and socially acceptable chit-chat? It has the right blend of exclusiveness and universality, as knowledge of the classics did, but is equally subject to the charge of being based on questionable ideals of the proper pursuits for ladies and gentlemen of leisure. One might argue that, if the point is just to have something to talk about, the exclusiveness is a doubtful virtue (given the diminishing height of class barriers) and the weather or the football pools might serve the purpose rather better.

Another possibility is that the labours and the triumphs of research might bring to spectators as well as participants some blend of the intellectual and aesthetic pleasures of discovery. Can laymen perhaps share in the achievements themselves in some sense that is significant, though vicarious? The honest answer must be that such sharing would rarely be much more than a matter of wishful identification with success, as with sailing round the world single-handed, or climbing Everest. It would not be very different really from the way the football fan thrills with pride when his chosen team wins the Cup. Not much better—and also, of course, no worse.

One thing is quite clear—that any cultural effects that science has must be exerted largely through the educational system. Yet the lines of justification we have considered so far do not carry overwhelming conviction that science warrants a place there. Everyone agrees, nevertheless, that it deserves a place, and many say that it should be a prominent one at that. Enthusiasts even maintain that education should be entirely science-based. Here is one strong statement of such a point of view: 'In the modern world, the only possible unified culture is a scientific culture, and the only adequate schooling is one built around science. Put right into the centre of things, science would not be narrow but comprehensive, and could restore to our educational system the coherence which it has not had since the classics lost their pre-eminence. Taught as it could be with six hours or more per week from the age of eight or nine, science would be a medium not only for the inculcation of scientific facts but also—and equally important—for the development of sensuous discriminations, the refinement of aesthetic appreciation and the attainment of clarity and grace in the use of the mother tongue as a means of exact communication'[28].

In considering the place of science in education, the need arises to make an important distinction. There are two fundamentally different things about science that could reach the world at large—its results on the one hand, and its methods and ways of thought on the other.

To the extent that the results of science are facts about the universe, and that science as taught consists of such 'nature-story' facts (section 2d), it is difficult to justify a special place for it in education. Facts worth teaching are so numerous that, whatever selection one makes, it is likely to score a very low success ratio in terms of pupils' future requirements. Faced with the problem of choosing teaching material, one is tempted to fall back on cynicism and rate all facts as equal. Most teachers nevertheless retain a residual faith that some facts are more equal than others.

The Teaching of Science

Perhaps scientific facts are, on average, more equal than the general run of other facts, but there is not much in it. Considered merely as information, there are certainly many non-scientific facts that should rank high in priority, and a great many scientific ones that must rank very low. Science can illuminate daily life; but how important is it really to have some picture of electrons whizzing when the electric light is switched on, or of the atoms that compose the fur in the kettle, or of the glands that are helping digest one's breakfast? These things add something to one's outlook, certainly, but whether they are a *sine qua non* for civilized existence is open to question.

Similarly when science is used to impress with the extraordinary rather than to explain the homely. The dimensions of the universe, or the number of molecules in a glass of water, may be at least as interesting and illuminating as the date of Magna Carta, but probably none of these is as eye-opening as the number of people killed in the two World Wars, or the rate of increase in world population.

e. SCIENCE AS A WAY OF THOUGHT

As a body of facts, then, science ranks quite high for teaching material, but not outstandingly so. There remains to be considered its value as a way of thought and as an intellectual discipline. How good a way is it to sharpen wits and develop mental skills?

Clearly, it has both advantages and disadvantages. The proper way to assess them, in theory, is to compare scientific subjects with others available in education.

It is sometimes said that scientific training, because it involves evaluating evidence and reaching objective conclusions, should develop powers of doing these things so that they can be used in other fields as well. With the best will in the world, it is difficult to see much educational reality in this. As far as school pupils and undergraduates are concerned, there is in practice lamentably little sifting and weighing of evidence anyway—they are kept too busy learning facts and principles. Conant[29] has argued that the professional tradition in which a scientist works is now so strong that it becomes almost automatic for him to be impartial and accurate in the laboratory. His instruments almost force it on him. But in the world outside, the problems of achieving impartiality and accuracy are often quite another matter. The nature of the evidence and of the conclusions wanted from it can look very different—or be more different than they look. That is why attempts to apply scientific method outside science are not without their pitfalls (section 2b).

A stronger point is that in science, especially in its more advanced branches, knowledge has reached an impressive degree of organization. Here is an area of inquiry where the systematization and codification of facts has reached a high level of power and sophistication. We can make some approach to imparting this merely by teaching science partly as principles rather than as isolated facts (see, however, sections 2e and 4d). Potentially at least, we are then teaching mental skills rather than mere facts, because we are illustrating effective methods of processing a multiplicity of raw data — ways of encapsulating facts in generalizations and thereby making them more manageable.

Clearly, this is one of the benefits of studying success. Success stories have some value as models for other kinds of intellectual endeavour, as long as they are used with due caution. One prerequisite for good teaching material is that good work should have been done in the area. It is in this that the principal strength of classical education lies—it deals with some of the finest thought in the history of mankind. A student of classics comes into contact with great minds through the medium of their writings (not only the classical authors themselves, but also some of those who have commented on them since). In science, the contact is less direct and less personal because—for several reasons, including some good ones—students rarely read the works of great scientists at first hand. What they study is nevertheless the product of great minds. The material is of high intellectual quality.

Success also has its drawbacks, though (section 2a). Dealing with areas where knowledge has reached a high degree of codification is not necessarily a good preparation for facing situations where the facts have to be coped with in their rawness and multiplicity. Most situations in real life are of this kind (hence the tension that can never entirely vanish between the simplified order of the world of scholarship and the confusing disorder of the world of action). Here the less advanced branches of science

The Teaching of Science

score somewhat in educational value over the more advanced branches, and history scores over both. The historian deals with facts in large numbers. Each fact individually is quite simple, even trivial in itself; the skill that is called into play lies in coping with them *en masse*, viewing them critically and selectively, ordering them and arguing a case with them in extended prose. (Possibly history of science can be made to combine many of the major advantages—see section 5k).

Connected closely with this is a point about the kind of reading that students do. Whatever they do in the way of 'outside' reading, the 'work' reading of science students tends to be largely confined to intensive study of a few textbooks. Students of arts subjects like history get more chance and encouragement to read extensively. They can better put into practice Bacon's admirable advice: 'Read not to contradict, nor to believe, but to weigh and consider. Some books are to be tasted, others to be swallowed, and some few to be chewed and digested"[30]. The unfortunate science student tends to be so busy chewing that he gets little chance to taste widely and to cultivate the important art of 'skimming' without missing the occasional nugget of gold that is relevant to the purpose in hand.

Another related point is this. Some people are put off science by the thought that all the answers are already known. This is very far from being true, of course, in any branch of science; but it can appear all too horribly true from the worm's eye view that a student gets. He is such an immense distance from the research front, his teacher knows such a vast amount more than he does, that to all intents and purposes it is a waste of time for him to argue. So there is a temptation to prefer a subject where he can get quickly to unsolved problems (curve A of the figure in section 2a). Partly this reflects undue haste on the part of impatient youth, but partly also a genuine, understandable and justified desire to exercise the critical and constructive as well as the absorptive and memorizing faculties of the mind.

There is one special case of the mind-training function of science that should be mentioned here, even though it clearly overlaps with the use of science for material benefits. It concerns numeracy, in the sense of a certain facility with basic mathematics. Numeracy has major uses these days outside natural science. It is heavily involved, for instance, in modern decision-making tools for management—for a variety of techniques covered by the umbrella name 'operations research', for making mathematical models to help planning and control, for optimizing production, distribution and marketing. Faith in such methods is growing—a fact on which much of the success of the Business Schools rests. Their experience, especially with the relatively mature students they get from industry, is that most of what they have to teach can be picked up quite easily provided only that there is a basis of some degree of facility with mathematics. It is those who have let their mathematics rust since their mid-teens who find it heavy going.

The pool of numeracy in the population, apart from mathematicians themselves, consists largely of those who trained as scientists. Natural scientists are no longer alone here; some types of social science training (though not all, by any means) are highly numerate, more so than many natural science courses. But, for obvious reasons, new activities have to be developed and manned initially by people trained in old subjects, and there is still a steady drift of people with natural science backgrounds turning their attention to social science problems.

The mathematics required for management and social science applications is commonly of only moderate sophistication. Specialist mathematicians with honours degrees in mathematics are often not required and not necessarily ideal. As a matter of historical fact, operations research was developed during the Second World War largely by groups of scientists. It may be that there is more significance in this fact than the sheer necessity of other numerate manpower not being available. Scientific training may have a value in its own right in that it shows real situations being treated mathematically to good effect. In other words, what success natural scientists have had in numerate social sciences they may owe not just to the fraction of their studies that they devoted to mathematics courses but also to the 'feel' for *using* mathematics that they got in science. There is a case to argue that the way to learn to use mathematics is to study physics, not mathematics. (There is also the analogous proposition that the way to learn to use English is to study history, not English. Should history be known as 'applied English'?)

There may be some other special cases besides numeracy of developing relatively specific skills[31]. In general, however, it

The Teaching of Science

must be admitted that our ideas about the relative educational values of subjects as mind-builders rest largely on faith; that is to say, we believe in them (as we do in many of the most important things) not because the evidence is so clear-cut and conclusive but despite the fact that it is not. Some types of education have, of course, acquired special prestige in the past, but the justification for this is not easy to assess. The major difficulty is the role of social convention. To point to the number of distinguished men who were educated in classics, say, proves nothing about the intrinsic educational virtues of that subject if it was the accepted convention forty years earlier that bright boys study classics. The best argument for studying classics in such a situation is that, if the convention is strong and longstanding, it is in classics that one is likely to find the best teachers, the best books and the best fellow-students. There is thus an element of the circle about it, vicious or otherwise. (Analogous considerations apply to other types of convention, such as the idea that French is 'more feminine' than physics.)

The relative educational virtues of subjects could perhaps in theory be assessed by their efficiency in preparing for 'general' careers—that is, careers not closely related to major subjects of study, where job contents are very different from course contents. In practice, however, it is barely possible to do this. Even with relatively vocational courses, it is difficult enough[32]. The verdicts of employers, employees and students are not conclusive; though valuable as items of evidence, they often overestimate the directness of the relation between aims and results, between the overt contents and objectives of education and the effects that it actually has (section 5b). There is, however, one slight wisp of evidence which is worth quoting.

The 'generalist' activity *par excellence* is administration. In the administrative grade of the British Civil Service, we have an administrative élite which is carefully selected by a highly developed procedure that claims to be independent of subject studied. It is possible to ask how graduates from different subjects fare in this career. 'For the benefit of the Fulton Committee, the Civil Service Commissioners made a survey of the performance of candidates at a later stage in their Civil Service careers. They found that when they were scored for rank achieved, present performance and promise, there was no significant

The Social Implications of Science

difference in their showing which could be related to subjects studied at the university. History, Greats, the natural sciences, English, economics, widely differing in content as they are, seem all one when it comes to success in the later career. One might deduce from this that all university courses are equally efficacious in training the mind'[33].

This conclusion needs qualifying in detail (section 4g) but there is no real case for denying its general validity.

f. SCIENCE FOR MATERIAL WELFARE

The question of harnessing science to bring material benefits is, like the question of science as culture, one where the main outlines are unmistakable but where the picture becomes the more complex and confusing the harder one looks. Obviously science *can* generate material benefits; but having said that, it is necessary to insist at once that it does not *necessarily* do so. The view that more science automatically leads to more wealth, however plausible it may seem as a first assumption, does not stand up to examination. It is not true for the individual, or for the nation, or for mankind.

For the individual, competence in science is nowadays a reasonable guarantee of a decent income. Genuine unemployment among scientists hardly exists, in most countries, at least. But anybody who wants to remain a scientist in any strict sense is virtually debarred from anything approaching the higher income brackets[34]. (Perhaps this is not a really serious injustice. Those who are really interested in money and get most satisfaction through it are free to occupy themselves in ways more directly concerned with it.)

For the nation and for mankind, the situation is more complex. It is now generally accepted that technological advance is a major contributor to economic growth. The extent of its contribution is difficult to determine at all exactly and remains a matter for debate among economists[35], but qualitatively the fact does not admit of much doubt.

However, the relation of technological advance to science is not simple and direct, and is not nearly as well understood as many people seem to imagine. The degree of dependence between these two processes (whether mutual or unilateral) is often over-emphasized. New technology builds to a large extent on earlier technology, just as new science builds on earlier science. Direct science-technology interaction — in the sense that a particular recent scientific discovery finds embodiment in successful technology—seems to be a relatively rare occurrence. Thus, in a study of a substantial number of recent outstandingly successful technological innovations, it has been possible in only a small minority of the cases to show any reasonably immediate connection with basic science[36].

What is probably a much more real effect is a much more diffuse one—namely, the way in which new technology draws on the general background of knowledge made available by science. Price[37] has suggested that much technology uses the science that is 'one generation of students' old. Obviously this cannot be more than a part of the whole story, but it is probably not entirely without foundation.

Notwithstanding the nebulous nature of the relation of basic science to technology, one might perhaps expect some correlation between applied research and increase in wealth, at least at the overall, macro-economic level, the level of national economies rather than individual firms. Even this expectation is not borne out in practice. In the national statistics on research and development expenditures, applied research and development heavily outweigh basic research, but even so, the proportions of their gross national products that different countries spend in these ways are not well correlated, by and large, with either wealth (gross national product per head) or growth (increase in output per head)[38].

Of course, increase in gross national product is not the sole and overriding aim of national policies. Much research and development work has no economic growth objective; there may be any degree of admixture of cultural or welfare or prestige or military considerations. Nobody suggests that in science policy, any more than in any other kind of national policy-making, we should become idolatrous worshippers at the shrine of the god of growth. Any such monotheism is quite inappropriate. But planning for wealth is nevertheless a legitimate and proper major aim of policy. Few people nowadays find poverty a spiritually uplifting state. On the national as well as the personal level, lack of resources limits the scope of action. It is miserable and humiliating not to be able to afford to do things that one feels are worth doing by quite non-materialist criteria. Since it is largely up to industry to create wealth (however we choose to run the industry and to share out the wealth once it has been created), there is thus at least a measure of truth in the saying that 'what's good for General Motors is good for the United States', and it might equally well be said that 'what's good for I.C.I. is good for Britain'.

That being so, it is worth looking at some more of the complexities of the relation of science to industry. The simple view which seems so plausible at first sight may be expressed as a linear model of the following type:

education→basic science→applied science→technology→wealth.

This makes it seem as though there is a simple causal chain. More education produces more scientists who create more scientific knowledge, more of which becomes applied in new technology which soon generates more wealth. I have already commented that the relation between scientific knowledge and technological know-how is not quite as simple as is implied by this. Now I want to point to another complication, which has to do with manpower. It concerns the distribution of scientific and technological manpower between different phases of the process.

Economists have argued that it is important to consider the alternative uses that are possible for trained scientists and technologists[39]. Since the total supply of such manpower is limited and cannot be changed quickly, putting too much effort into one sector may be not merely useless but could actually *hinder* growth by depleting another sector. If so, a simple interpretation of the linear model could be positively misleading.

There are two likely bottlenecks where it seems that shortages may be pinching and limiting the overall process. Firstly, excessive emphasis on finding new knowledge might lead to insufficient attention being paid to finding applications latent in the knowledge already available; the main failure may be not in creating new science but in using existing science—in other words, not in increasing the *size* of the stock of knowledge but in improving our *utilization* of it. Secondly, even applied research and development may be excessive if the output of new technology is greater than industry's capacity profitably to

The Teaching of Science

absorb it, provided that the absorptive capacity could be increased by more scientific and technological awareness outside the research and development function itself—in planning, production and marketing, for instance, as well as in 'general management'.

The pertinence of the first of these lines of argument clearly depends on the existing balance of the efforts in pure and applied science and on the transferability of skills between these two sectors. The pertinence of the second depends on the extent to which scientific and technological knowledge and skills are useful outside the research and development function. These two questions are important, and it is principally to them that most of the rest of this chapter is devoted. The more closely one looks at them, the more complex they become. (Indeed, the relation of science to wealth can be taken as a particularly pointed illustration of Oscar Wilde's dictum that 'the truth is rarely pure and never simple'.)

g. BALANCE BETWEEN BASIC AND APPLIED SCIENCE

I have already alluded to the preference that scientists quite often show for the purer over the more applied kinds of science (section 2f). This tendency seems to be more marked in Britain than in some other countries, and is more pronounced than mere head-counting might indicate because it takes effect specially among those with the highest qualifications and ability. It is due partly to social convention but partly also to an inevitable difference in primary motivation between the educational and industrial sectors coupled with the natural tendency of students to take on the attitudes of their teachers. Perhaps there is a need here for a few latter-day successors to Francis Bacon, combining his kind of fiery vision with the literary gifts to convey it to others so as to make applied science intellectually and morally more respectable. If only 'great books' could be commissioned, industry might make a good investment in commissioning a few on science in industry.

One source of difficulty is that much industrial application uses relatively old and simple science. There are, of course, exceptions to this—in solid state physics, for instance—and in such areas there is a strong case for industry to keep in good contact with up-to-date university research and to recruit high-quality Ph.D.s primed with the brightest and newest ideas and techniques. But in large sectors of industry, it is very much down-to-earth, bread-and-butter science that is mostly used—not the stuff that is acquired doing a research degree, not even the contents of the final Honours year, but the basic material of the earlier stages of scientific education[40].

That does not mean that it is right to look down one's nose at it and dismiss it as dull and routine. It is true, undoubtedly, that many scientists in industry are given dull and routine jobs, and this is a genuine failure of management, but it is not fair to assume without further ado that they are 'underemployed' just because they are not using the latest news from the research front in glamour areas of basic science. It is quite wrong to suppose that, as soon as any new discovery is published, the applied scientists fall on it in their hordes and squeeze every drop of application out of it in a few years. They could not possibly do so, even if there were more of them and they tried harder than they do. A fact that has been lying around useless for years may suddenly become vital as knowledge advances on other fronts; and in any case, the needs to be filled by applying science change as society changes. In a way, even more credit is due for finding a new use for a fact thirty or even a hundred years old than for applying one from last month's research paper. But currently prevalent notions of what carries prestige do not often seem to take this view[41].

A similar difficulty concerning prestige arises from the role of imitation in innovation. At first sight, on a common sense analysis, it may seem that an innovation can be made for the first time only once, and that all subsequent uses of it—from which, if they are at all numerous, the bulk of the economic benefits must usually come—are mere imitations which present no scientific or technological challenge. However, even to copy something demands some degree of understanding of it, and if it is complicated this requires ability and training. Furthermore, novelty is not an all-or-none phenomenon. Imitations are rarely exact; innovations, on the other hand, always have antecedents of some kind, however indirect; so there is a continuous range of degrees of novelty between the two extremes (just as there is for scientific discoveries—see section 2e). An imitation of a process

The Teaching of Science

from another firm in the same industry rates only a low degree of originality. But to utilize a type of process or technique developed in a different industrial technology may be a genuinely creative act. It may require great acumen to see the opportunity in the first place, and then considerable technical skill to push the necessary modifications to a successful conclusion. Such 'technology transfer' seems to be an important source of technical progress[42].

In applied science, the *source* of knowledge is not important. What matters is its successful *application*. Thus, on both the national and on the company levels, there is a case for resisting the pressures that arise out of notions about prestige to regard 'home-grown' knowledge as in some way superior to the imported product[43]. A great deal of knowledge is freely and internationally available. The course that so often pays off is to wait poised until a field is almost ripe for successful application and then to leap in and energetically take the last few steps needed to reap the fruit; or—to vary the metaphor—to hang back until the finishing line is in sight and then to sprint. This demands personnel very much on the alert to what is going on, keen to see opportunities and prepared to jump at them when they appear, instead of plodding along their own chosen lines. (Bacon had a point when he assigned a third of his top-grade scientific manpower to be Merchants of Light, charged with the job of keeping track of developments abroad rather than possibly duplicating them at home—see section 3c.) An object-lesson is provided by Du Pont, an American firm noted for its technical progressiveness. Of the twenty-five innovations examined in a recent study, only ten were based on discoveries attributable to Du Pont's own employees[44].

As regards the transferability of manpower from pure to applied science, the general point can be made with some confidence that *skill* is often quite easily transferable; the difficulty is commonly one of *motivation*. Most good physicists could have made good engineers, and most good academic chemists good industrial ones, if only they had wanted. I say this quite without prejudice to my recurring theme that applied science is not just an inferior and adulterated version of the pure product (sections 2f, 3h, 5b). Its demands are not less but different, smaller in some directions but greater in others. There must, notably, be not only a willingness to consider a wider range of factors as relevant but also the ability to assess them and draw the right conclusions from them.

Possibly some of the distrust of 'outside' factors that is sometimes felt in scientific circles can be traced to excesses elsewhere in the past. Thus, in the notorious Lysenko affair, the distortion of genetics in Russia during the nineteen-forties (section 3b), one important factor at issue was emphasis on practical utility. The relatively fixed and unchanging nature of hereditary characters in Mendelian genetics implied to the Lysenko school that crop plants cannot be rapidly improved, and this kind of defeatism they refused to accept. On a much higher plane scientifically, Ashby records the case of the distinguished Russian botanist, N. P. Krenke, and comments on 'the emphasis which he laid upon the practical application of his results, using this pragmatic test almost as though the validity of his experiments depended on their utility'[45].

In most cases, however, there are no such sinister implications and it is not honest doubt but lack of will that prevents scientists from making themselves more 'user-oriented'. As an illustration that it *can* be done in Britain, the record of scientists in the Second World War is sometimes quoted. It is a fine record—they seem rarely to have missed a trick—and part of the reason must be that some of the usual difficulties of motivation did not apply. There was no fear of being tainted by sordid commerciality; it was all part of the war effort to which the nation was devoting itself with rare unanimity and single-mindedness. So scientists were prepared to emerge from their splendid isolation and to develop regular close contacts with potential users. A. P. Rowe, who was concerned with the development of radar, recalls that, at the Telecommunications Research Establishment, Malvern, regular meetings were arranged between the 'boffins' and the military personnel who were going to use the devices being developed. 'And so to T.R.E. on Sundays came senior officers of the Royal Air Force (sometimes Commanders-in-Chief), junior officers fresh from operations, top headquarters people and scientists from other establishments or engaged on operational research'[46].

Some of the internal strains and stresses of physics in the nineteen-sixties are symptomatic and illustrate the complexities of the issues involved. The dominance of nuclear physics is criticized by some as reflecting a 'preoccupation of physics with itself'[47]. The giant particle accelerators already in operation are enormously expensive to build and run, and even bigger ones are proposed (section 3d). In fact, physics has become a major *consumer* of money. Is it, then, actually acting more as a sponge than as a fount of wealth? Is this a case of private affluence amid public squalor—the nuclear physicists getting exorbitantly expensive toys while others have to go without much more basic requirements? Are accelerators actually counterproductive in economic terms because of the way they suck up money and men?

It is not easy to answer questions like these because of a number of uncertainties, one of which is this. The amount of nuclear physics proper that goes into building and operating these machines is really quite a small proportion of the total effort. An enormous quantity of high-grade engineering has to be built around the initial gleam in a nuclear physicist's eye. Much of the actual experimental work deals with severely practical problems of instrumentation and so forth. Nuclear physics should, therefore, provide a good training ground for men to do applied physics in industry. At least, it could do so in theory; whether it works that way in practice is more questionable.

h. AWARENESS OF SCIENCE OUTSIDE THE LABORATORY

So much for the vexed question of 'turning scientists more applied'. But the alternative posed by the basic-applied dichotomy is not the only one that has to be taken into account in considering the deployment of scientific and technological skills in the complex process of creating wealth from knowledge. After all—still keeping for the moment to the British national scene—it is difficult to argue that there have been glaring overall deficiencies in either the quantity or the intrinsic quality of applied science in the recent past. It has not been neglected, nor has it been bad in the sense that there have been no good brains in it. One cannot pin much of the blame for our lack of economic success on any failure of applied science in itself.

The point that remains to be discussed is the usefulness of scientific and technological knowledge and skills outside the research and development function in any strict sense—that is, scientific awareness outside the laboratory. In general terms (the full extent of their generality will emerge in the next section), this usefulness lies in performing 'integrating' functions. It is sometimes said that the development of a specialist function often brings with it the need for a corresponding integrating function to tie it in with other activities and aims of society. Science, as a supreme example of a major, highly specialized activity, provides an outstanding case of such a need.

In the industrial context, the problem can be at least partly identified with what has been called the 'management gap'. In so far as there is some kind of 'gap' between the United States and Britain, so it is argued, it is not so much a technological gap as a managerial one.

It may be as well to consider in the first place what people with scientific or technological qualifications *actually* do in industry (irrespective of how good or bad the present balance is). There is a widespread misconception that scientists in industry are all wearing laboratory overalls and are tucked away in research laboratories. This is far from being the case. Many of them are more likely to be wearing white collars than white overalls.

Some figures on the actual proportions are available from the 1965 manpower survey[48]. Of the 127,000 qualified scientists and engineers identified as employed in industry, more than two-thirds are shown as engaged on work other than research and development (nearly half the scientists, and about three-quarters of the engineers and technologists). These proportions are almost certainly underestimates, because only about two-thirds of the total estimated manpower stock was accounted for, and because firms like to emphasize their research activity, for reasons of prestige among others, and therefore tend to class as research some activities about which others might have doubts. (There is a story of a large science-based firm which conducted a use of time survey among its employees; one instruction for filling up the forms was, if in doubt, call it R and D.)

Some people seem to interpret these figures as signs of 'underemployment'. Rather as in the case of the other kind of alleged underemployment—not letting scientists use their most up-to-date knowledge (section 3g)—this charge is certainly justified in some cases, but not in all. It is justified where qualified men are doing lowly, humdrum and routine work; but it is not necessarily justified in other cases, because genuine uses exist for scientific and technological backgrounds outside research and development, in other functions included under the general heading 'management'.

A major function of management in an industry that employs research workers must be the setting of suitable objectives for their work. It is often said that scientists must be given freedom if they are to work effectively, and so they must, but it is also undoubtedly the case that many scientists like being set a goal to work towards. As long as the goal seems clear and attainable, they often respond well to the challenge.

The task of management, therefore, is to present realistic challenges and to make them seem worth while. This is not just a matter of the management of research and development considered in a restricted sense as one of the several functions of a firm. Rather, it pervades much of its 'general management'—the more so, the more science-based the activities of the firm are. It includes production, and solving the technical problems that arise in this connection; for the line between development and production is often a hazy one. It also includes marketing, which may itself have a high technical content and through which awareness of consumer requirements is fed into the firm. Above all, it includes planning to meet those requirements, often to a distant time horizon.

Setting the proper goals for research and development, therefore, demands more than a knowledge of the scientific and technological possibilities. It cannot be done effectively by a scientist, however distinguished, as long as he remains totally a scientist. The decisions to be made have to take into account all the great variety of external pressures and needs as well as the technical possibilities for meeting them to all degrees and combinations of degrees. The larger the undertaking, the more difficult this task becomes—and the more crucial. It is no good exercising brilliant talents on developing new aeroplanes or atomic power plants if it then turns out that they are too big or too small or too noisy or too expensive or that they have in any of the multitude of possible ways the wrong performance characteristics for people to want them. No wealth is created thereby — quite on the contrary. In the nature of the case, the largest projects are usually financed mainly through Governments, not private industry, and Governments do not automatically go out of business when they fail to show profits[49]. So 'big technology' can outdo 'big science' in sucking up money and men, with all the same potentialities for counterproductiveness and much weaker 'cultural' justifications. Apparently useless knowledge surely deserves more sympathy than apparently useless technological hardware.

It is sometimes said, in such cases, that the research was good but that the end-product could not be put to use because economic or social or commercial factors were not propitious. There is some confusion of criteria here. Economic, social and commercial factors are not totally extraneous to the process of applied research; they are not of the nature of unpredictable 'acts of God' which the people responsible could not possibly have been expected to consider. So it cannot truly be said to be 'good' research, however much technical skill and ingenuity went into it. Of course, the final outcome depends to some extent on luck. It is not possible to know for certain in advance about political upheavals in foreign countries which might cut off supplies of some raw material, or what the exact patent position will be, or whether the market will shrink because of some change in consumer preferences, or whether the market will be captured altogether by some new technology. But these are areas where chances have to be assessed and where luck and judgment overlap. In this respect, the situation is just the same as in pure science (section 2c) except that the range of factors that has to be assessed is greater. It shows one way in which applied research can be more and not less demanding than pure. A greater number of factors, differing more widely from each other, has to be weighed and condensed into a synoptic view.

These complicating factors have to be added to the increasing complexity of the research process itself and the growing sophistication of its tools to give some indication of the range of skills that is required nowadays to generate successful discoveries and inventions on anything other than a pot-luck basis. It is hardly surprising that corporate research by teams seems to be overtaking private individuals in the output of inventions[50].

The problem thus arises of how to generate the right kind of 'skill mix'. To what extent can it be done by putting different specialists together round a conference table or a dinner table, or organizing them so that they mix at work, or making sure that they regularly drink coffee (or, better, beer) together? It has to be remembered here that the problem is to mix scientific and technological specialist skills not only with each other but also with non-scientific skills. For instance, the kind of multi-disciplinary project team that is now quite fashionable might include, say, in a small-scale example, a marketing man besides a chemist and two engineers of different kinds. In a group such as this, there has to be a positive and active willingness to co-operate —to give as well as take in terms of requirements, and to take as well as to give in terms of information. Otherwise the skills are just jumbled up together, not blended with each other.

Genuine blending is difficult to achieve. It sometimes seems as hard truly to mix different skills (and especially non-scientific with scientific ones) as it is to mix the boys and the girls at a school dancing class. They tend to separate out like oil and water when there is no emulsifying agent present to keep them mixed. Emulsifying agents—to carry the analogy one step further—are molecules in which one part has an affinity for oil and the other an affinity for water; they sit in the interface between the oil and the water and hold the two together, so to speak. Similarly with different skills. At least some of the individual persons must be willing and able to come out of the shells of their own specialisms and develop a part-affinity for others.

Similarly again when one goes from the level of the project team to that of the Board of Directors. It used to be fashionable to suggest that the way to make better use of science is to put one or two scientists or technologists on the Board. But Carter and Williams, in their deservedly famous study[51], found that the matter is not as simple as that. A scientist on the Board is no guarantee even of technical progressiveness, let alone commercial profitability. The capacity of an undertaking profitably to absorb technological innovation depends on a more subtle blend of technical and other factors than is automatically achieved merely by adding a scientific expert to the usual set of commercial ones.

The key question around which the issue revolves is the *degree of separability* of scientific and non-scientific considerations. If they are separable, then it is enough to rely on specialist technical advice. Management could first formulate the commercial objectives of the firm and then take specialist advice about how to achieve them. This is the philosophy of the scientist 'on tap but not on top'—providing a specialist service available to the decision-making process but not a part of it. If, however, the formulation of objectives must (or should) itself include technical factors as one of the formative ingredients of the decision-making process, then the solution is not quite so straightforward.

This latter type of situation seems to be quite common and important in science-based industry. It seems that, in so far as it is possible to trace commercially successful innovations meaningfully to a single source, that source is rarely a new discovery; sometimes it is recognition of a new need which can be met by a technical capability that already exists in its essentials; but most frequently it is the linking of an existing commercial need with an existing technical capability[52]. In such cases, the crucial event that determines what a firm should do is of necessity and intrinsically multidisciplinary. A loose juxtaposition of different ways of thought is not enough, because it is not just a case of one helping the other; the very essence lies in the combination.

i. INTEGRATING FUNCTIONS

With this issue of separability in mind, we can now begin to see the full generality and significance that attaches to 'integrating functions'. Clearly the concept does not apply only to industrial situations. The philosophy of the scientist 'on tap but not on top' originated not in industry but in politics (the phrase is Winston Churchill's). If it means merely that it would be bad to 'put scientists in charge' generally, then most reasonable people will agree readily enough. But if it is interpreted to mean that science can safely be left to the backroom boys, then it is dangerous, and the dangers have been pointed in a political context. Thus Bagrit, for instance, has called for 'science-orientated humanists' to be at the head of affairs in the Civil Service and politics as well as in industry, commerce and the trade unions[53]; and D. K. Price has pointed to the need for a kind of 'intellectual broker' to act as middleman between the realms of science and politics[54].

One of the most persuasive voices is that of Conant who, with the traumatic experience of war-time decisions on atom bombs behind him, pleaded eloquently for 'assimilating science into our cultural pattern'[55]. This takes us clearly quite beyond the question of science for material benefits. The issue now spreads back into that of science and culture. It is, in fact, much the same as that which C. P. Snow[56] labelled the problem of the 'two cultures'. The analysis into two cultures can be criticized easily enough—it is obviously very much oversimplified—but the way the debate caught on and spread like wildfire shows that it must have caught something that lay latent in many people's thinking.

One significant thing about the debate is that it originated in England. This is significant because it is here that the educational origins of the problem are clearest. The notoriously early specialization in the English educational system means that the gulf between scientists and non-scientists is that much wider—or, at least, the cleft between them goes deeper by two or three years of education. There have been many suggestions and some initiatives for educational ventures to 'cross the Snow line', but none has made a major impact so far.

The social effects of the arts-science gap are quite exceptionally difficult to pin down precisely. A major feature of the educational system is so deep-rooted and pervasive a cause that its effects must be multifarious and widespread. But one may at least wonder—is it purely a coincidence that Britain is an outstanding case of a country where good science, and plenty of it, co-exists with a depressingly low rate of economic growth? Or is there, perhaps, some causal connection? Could some large-scale failure of integrating functions be at least partly to blame?

People to perform integrating functions have to have both scientific and non-scientific background, interests and skills (on the model of the surface-active molecules that act as emulsifying agents). Since it is in general far harder to pick up science than non-science, this restricts the field essentially to those who started with a scientific training. The effectiveness with which this source can meet the demand depends on how much of an 'apparent surplus' of scientists there is—a surplus, that is, over and above those who remain in the specialist function for which they were specifically trained[57]. If the pressure of the apparent surplus is not strong, then all that is left for the integrating functions are the 'drop-outs', the 'failed' research workers and

The Social Implications of Science

those who have shot their bolts and are now past it (section 4h). So there is, here again, a question of quality superimposed on the bare numbers, and the situation cannot be properly assessed by mere head-counting. Integrating functions demand sets of skills and types of temperament that are not always the same as those that make for success in the laboratory; but they are not so insignificant or undemanding that they can safely be left to second-raters.

So the question is raised whether the educational system should more explicitly recognize the range and importance of the social implications of science. Clearly this is intimately tied up with the problem of specialization, and it is this issue which the next chapter takes up.

CHAPTER FOUR

SPECIALIZATION

a. THE NATURE OF THE PROBLEM

Specialization is the central issue in the teaching of science. Having examined both the scientific process itself and its social implications, the stage is now set for discussing it. How much specialization do we want, and in what ways and in what circumstances do we want it, to meet the various needs as indicated by the foregoing considerations?

The dilemma is posed in its broadest outlines—though not by any means in all its very real complexities and ramifications—by the conflicting requirements raised by chapters 2 and 3. On the one hand, the great amount and the high degree of intellectual sophistication of the knowledge built up over a long period of cumulative progress demands specialization to master an area and to get to the research front to make a contribution. So barriers of exclusiveness rise around sciences, with notices saying effectively, 'non-specialists keep out'. (Largely this is unintentional, of course; it is a more or less inevitable consequence of the advanced state of the subject-matter.) On the other hand, the influence of science outside itself is now immensely pervasive and potent[1]. This demands that scientists and the rest of society should be genuinely aware of each other. The intimacy of the intermingling between scientific and non-scientific considerations in the industrial, political and other spheres means both that laymen must take notice of science and that scientific specialists must be sensitive to outside factors.

There are many complications and overtones, but that seems to be the fundamental dilemma. In England and Wales, where the educational system favours rather intense specialization at a particularly early age—uniquely so, apparently, at least as far

Specialization

as Western Europe and North America are concerned—the issue has become a sort of bogey from which we seem unable to escape. To condemn the present degree of specialization as excessive has become quite a vogue, though not the universally accepted orthodoxy.

The key area in which the battle is joined is the sixth form curriculum; but the implications go further both up and down the educational system. There are indications that 'directional limitations' in combinations of subjects taken commonly begin to operate about two years before the sixth form[2], so that many pupils begin to become trams instead of buses at ages as early as 13 to 14. In the upward direction, the problems overlap with those of undergraduate courses both because of the question of university entry requirements and standards and because many of the considerations apply in an analogous way to university education itself, though naturally with different emphases[3].

The salient facts of the system in operation are these. Most pupils at English and Welsh schools study only arts or only science subjects seriously after the age of 15-16. Having taken a broader range for the 'O' level examinations at about that age[4], they concentrate on a small number of subjects during the two to three years that they spend in the sixth form. In the 'A' level examinations at the end of the sixth form career, the number of subjects taken is commonly three for those who have hopes of going on to university, and those three are usually chosen either entirely from the science side or entirely from the arts side[5,6].

The reservation is sometimes made that to consider only examination subjects gives a misleading picture. Some schools devote about one-third of the time-table to non-examination work, often called 'minority time' work or 'General Studies'. In form and content this work is, in the nature of the case, very variable—much of the point of the exercise is to give latitude to individual schools and teachers by freeing them from the constraints of examination syllabuses[7]. The best schools often take this work most seriously; they get their good examination results despite the time taken for it. Run-of-the-mill schools tend to feel that they cannot afford much time for it, perhaps because they have to struggle for their 'A' levels.

The Teaching of Science

The General Studies concept has a lot to recommend it, but it is sheer wishful thinking to suppose that it does all that is necessary to solve the problems of breadth in education. The seriousness of purpose with which it is tackled, both by teachers and by pupils, varies widely. Normally it includes work not primarily academic in purpose, such as religious instruction and physical education (physical jerks, not physical science). The proportion of one-third agreed by some schools is a proportion of the timetable, and it overestimates the proportion of a pupil's effort when private study and homework are taken into account[8]. Finally, and not surprisingly, General Studies are much less good at bringing some genuine science to arts specialists than *vice versa*.

Examinations have their weaknesses, heaven knows (the ones referred to in section 2d are not the only ones, or the ones most apparent to those who set, take and mark them); but they have their virtues too, even if examinees are less well placed to appreciate them before the event than after. They do act as powerful incentives. One is reminded of Dr Johnson's remark about hanging: 'Depend upon it, Sir, when a man knows he is to be hanged in a fortnight, it concentrates his mind wonderfully'. An examination is not quite as drastic as hanging, but it does exert the effort-focusing effect of a forthcoming crisis; and without some focusing of effort, not much of value can be got from studying science.

So there is no getting around it—most sixth formers devote their energies, with a high degree of exclusiveness, to a relatively narrow area, and in particular to one side only of the arts-science boundary. That is the time-honoured English system, and there are still plenty of people who feel in no mood to condemn it or even apologize for it. They exult in it, and point to the high level of sixth form work at its best as one of the glories of English education[9].

Perhaps the most notable defence of the system in recent years came in the Crowther Report of 1959. 'After considering the matter most carefully', concluded its distinguished authors, 'we are agreed in accepting and endorsing the English principle of specialization'[10].

Yet within a few years of this verdict being delivered with such deliberation, the climate of opinion changed drastically.

Specialization

Just a few of the symptoms that have appeared in print will suffice here. The respected scientific journal *Nature* in 1967 sponsored a conference whose distinguished participants from varied backgrounds agreed 'that a broadening of the curriculum in the sixth form is an urgent need'[11]. The semi-official Schools Council, in its proposals for sixth form work in 1966 (the major-minor scheme) and 1967 (the two 'A' levels plus electives scheme) expressly declared the intention to counteract excessive specialization (though in the latter case there was some doubt whether the scheme proposed would actually have that effect)[12]. Easily the most weighty of all, the Dainton Report appeared with a mass of statistical and other supporting evidence in 1968; its summary of recommendations begins by declaring flatly, 'there should be a broad span of studies in the sixth forms'[13].

b. THE LURE OF RESEARCH

From the point of view of science, one of the attractions of early specialization is that it lets young people get on to research as quickly as possible. They can be given a chance to do something creative and original before hardening of the brain sets in. After all, nobody wants the eternal student, even for an academic career.

The lure of research is certainly one of the biggest incentives for the young to study science. In a survey made in 1961, an overwhelmingly large proportion of sixth form boys on the science side gave research as the first choice of ultimate career[14]. The main reason given was that it is 'exciting'. Now it is true, of course, that the schoolboy's image of the research scientist may be much over-glamourized, and his expectation of ever becoming one may be quite unrealistic; but there is nevertheless a spark of something genuine and important in this. Visions of standing at the frontier of knowledge, of finding out something that nobody has ever known before, of making a major invention, of the ultimate accolade of scientific honours, of honorary degrees and fellowships of societies and Nobel prizes — these dream-ambitions are not to be lightly brushed aside. No one wants to choke off the enthusiasm of the young. So, however misplaced or misguided their impatience, it would be a shame for their more cynical elders to make the path to research into an obstacle-race strewn with irrelevant hurdles. All that should be done is to temper enthusiasm with the fruits of experience.

For the future practising scientist, of course, the question is not *whether* to specialize, but only when, how much and in what ways. Specialize he must, sooner or later, to become professionally effective, whether in the academic sphere or the industrial.

There is a view which is widely current—though it derives more from the introspective reminiscences of scientists than from serious socio-psychological study — which might be called the 'hour-glass theory' of the development of a scientific career. According to this view, the natural pattern of development is somewhat as follows. The range of a person's interests starts wide, with the catholic tastes of youth; in the late teens and early twenties, it narrows while all energies are concentrated on achieving something in a first piece of research; then it broadens out again with the maturity of age. This picture does seem to correspond roughly to the actual experience of many. Whether things would have turned out better or worse some other way, and at what age the constriction is best put in, and how narrow it is best to make it, and how big the differences are between individuals—these are wide open questions. There seems to be no sound basis on which to judge.

Plenty of room for debate therefore remains. It is still not settled how much non-scientific education a budding scientist should have; how extensive a basic groundwork he should be given to make him successful in research or professional practice, bearing in mind the long run as well as the short; and whether he should perhaps specialize on more than one front so that he can bring some non-standard combination of skills and background to bear and possibly achieve some breakthrough with a pincer movement of creative bisociation (section 2e).

An oft-recurring question raises its argumentative head again here. How far should education go in aiming to match in content the demands of particular sets of existing jobs? To what extent is it better for the educator to content himself with merely tilling the soil and not sowing specific seeds?

Putting people into jobs other than those for which their formal education specifically prepared them reflects what is sometimes called the 'substitutability' of skills, but this is

Specialization

partially misleading; the point at issue is not just the extent to which students and their eventual employers (whether industrial or academic) can make do with something not accurately tailor-made but also the extent to which it might be a positive advantage to bring new ranges and combinations of knowledge and experience to bear. There is a great deal to be said in favour of changing tracks even within the realm of academic research. Notable successes have been scored by transitions such as physics graduates going into some branch of the life sciences, or chemistry graduates into computer work. There is virtue in making the effort to become a bus again after having been, to all appearances, a tram. Adaptability may pay. In a somewhat similar way, those engineering employers whose horizons of vision extend more than a year or two ahead have come to condemn too much specialization into different types of engineering at undergraduate level, on the grounds that, although it may be immediately useful, it can decrease adaptability to changing circumstances in the long run.

Furthermore, scope for adaptability extends not only through but also beyond the range of technical functions. In the recruiting literature of large science-based firms one can sometimes find tabulated the kinds of jobs for which various kinds of graduates are considered suitable. Commonly, a physics degree offers the greatest number of options, covering managerial as well as a range of technical functions. Care is needed in interpreting this fact. Partly it is due, beyond doubt, to the fact that physics happens to attract a good share of talented boys, and it does not necessarily mean that everything in existing physics courses is exactly right just the way it is. What it is more likely to mean is this. Few if any of the specialist activities of the firm correspond at all closely to the contents of physics courses; so, as far as the firm is concerned, a physics degree is *not* specialized—it is just an education of a vaguely relevant kind.

The value of this lies partly in the fact that the effect of specialization is as much on motivation as on skill. A specialized graduate tends to *want* to practise his specialism—otherwise he feels he is 'wasting' his education[15]. A physics graduate in industry thus has a certain advantage in this respect over a graduate in some restricted sub-branch of engineering, and this does something to offset his lack of immediately useful skills.

The Teaching of Science

This leads on to a still wider point. For many students taking science, the question how much to specialize almost becomes a question of whether to specialize at all. Genuine research workers — people who make their careers predominantly in laboratories—look like continuing to form a minority of the output of scientific education. However important the minority, however many of the most gifted it includes (for better or for worse, for richer or for poorer), however much one wants to avoid levelling down for the sake of the rest, it still remains the case that the rest are not there merely for the sake of the minority. To argue by a *reductio ad absurdum*: the scale of our effort in science teaching should not merely reflect the necessary inefficiency of producing one Nobel prizewinner a year (which is roughly Britain's recent average).

Here again, it is possible that the choices people make may reflect social conventions as much as individual interests and inclinations. Once the idea gets around that all the brightest people stay at university after taking a first degree to do three years' research and get a Ph.D. for it, then to do just that becomes a way for a young man to show to himself, to his friends and to his potential employers that he is one of the brightest people. So it is at least possible that there may be research students whose existence in universities is not very strongly justified either by their urge and ability to contribute significantly to knowledge, or by the value of a research degree as training over and above the value of other kinds of experience that they might be accumulating during those very formative years. Consequently, the 'argument from research' in favour of early specialization may not apply quite as widely or with quite as much weight as is sometimes supposed.

c. SOCIO-PSYCHOLOGICAL CONSIDERATIONS

Another line of argument is that young minds at the age of 15 to 16 want to specialize and that they are ready for it, so that to let them is good in that it lets nature take its proper course, whereas to prevent them is artificial coercion. Perhaps it is just possible that the population of England and Wales is different in this respect from that of the rest of Western Europe and North America, but it seems unlikely (at least from the stand-

Specialization

point of individual rather than social psychology). Alternatively, it may be not the young people who are different but the educationists who have been cleverer, having recognized an important fact and acted on it in building a system that exploits it. That argument is much more difficult to assess one way or the other.

The Crowther Report naturally used it. 'Subject-mindedness is one of the marks of the sixth form', its authors maintained, and they contended that it should be exploited since it is there anyway[16]. There is a curious boomerang quality about the argument, though. Three paragraphs later we are told that one reason for letting 16-year-olds indulge their alleged 'subject-mindedness' is that they may then have grown out of it by the age of 18. The authors clearly felt able to place the constriction in the hourglass (section 4b) rather specifically in the age range 16 to 18. How often the process of broadening out again at 18 really takes place is open to question; with a few exceptions—very few indeed on the science side—university courses provide little encouragement for it. Certainly the picture does not quite tally with that of the get-on-to-research-quickly school of thought, which places the narrowest phase in the early twenties.

The Dainton committee recognized the importance of the issue and commissioned a survey of the literature on it[17] which is drawn on in their Report[18]. There is a fair amount of evidence to support the impressions that anyone could get from everyday experience that 'fairly stable vocational interests' often begin to emerge at a young age, and that it is quite common for science *versus* non-science differentiation to be reasonably well established by the early teens. Uncertainties about a number of important points remain, and are difficult to resolve. It is not clear, for instance, how strong the differentiation is in how large a proportion of the population, and how far the educational system determines the nature, the timing and the irrevocability of the choices rather than the other way round.

Even if the evidence were a good deal more decisive than it is, we would still have to beware of using it in a quite unjustified way for planning the shape of education. The fact that differences in tastes and abilities do exist is in itself a weak argument—hardly an argument at all, really—for giving up any particular subject at any particular age. There are plenty of children who show unmistakably at primary school that they have greater interest and ability in English than in mathematics, or the other way round; but it would be wrong to conclude that they should give up one subject or the other on entering secondary school at the age of eleven.

There is one recent study on psychological biases which is so attractive, so easy to read and so delightful to discuss that it may be exerting an undue influence. It is Hudson's *Contrary Imaginations*[19]. Hudson takes up the distinction made by earlier workers between 'high I.Q.' and 'high creative' children and renames the groups 'convergers' and 'divergers' respectively. Convergers are good at intelligence tests where most items have only one right answer, arrived at by logical reasoning; divergers are good at 'open-ended' tests of the type, 'how many uses can you think of for a brick?' The distinction shows signs of passing in exaggerated form into folk culture. From the way it is talked about sometimes, one might think that in the beginning He created them convergers and divergers rather as He made them male and female.

The fault is not Hudson's, for he presents his evidence carefully. (Perhaps his book is more spoken about than read, despite its readability.) It should be enough here to note just two points from it.

Firstly, it is important to remember that what nature presents is, as so often, a continuous distribution; the boundaries are imposed on this by man's urge to make distinctions and to classify. Hudson says, 'as a matter of convenience, I define 30 per cent of my usual schoolboy sample as convergers, 30 per cent as divergers, and leave the remaining 40 per cent in the middle as all-rounders. For the most part, my results are expressed in terms of comparisons between the two extreme groups, convergers and divergers. If at times the all-rounders seem neglected, this is not because they are unimportant, but because comparisons between contrasting groups are a convenient way of describing complex results'[20].

Secondly, it is important to bear in mind what kind of differences were found between groups. They seem quite genuine, but they are small compared to the spread of the groups and their overlap (and that, it must be remembered, in tests designed to show differences). Thus the table of sixth form subjects chosen[21] gives the following figures.

Specialization

	Extreme Divergers	Mild Divergers	All-Rounders	Mild Convergers	Extreme Convergers
History	7	15	17	3	2
Modern Languages	3	18	26	7	0
Mixed Courses	4	1	14	4	0
Classics	1	2	3	7	3
Physical Science	3	12	33	37	19
Biology	1	4	14	4	3

A glance at this table shows that to say that convergers and divergers correspond to the science and arts sides in sixth forms is a very gross oversimplification indeed.

It may help, in trying to put Hudson's study into perspective, to consider the type of approach it adopts. Analysis in terms of pairs of opposites is a time-honoured procedure when nothing better is available. Chemical speculation started that way; the Greeks chose the pairs hot-cold and moist-dry to define the 'elements' in terms of which they classified the properties of different substances. Nobody improved appreciably on that until Lavoisier's gravimetric analyses and Dalton's atomic theory, more than 2,000 years later; but once the more satisfactory basis for chemical theory had been found, the feebleness of the old one was soon very apparent. Within the field of psychological types, we have already had, in this century, William James's tender-minded and tough-minded, and Jung's extrovert and introvert. The converger-diverger distinction is the latest in this fascinating tradition to catch on, but it is unlikely to be the last word on the subject. It makes an admirable basis for semi-intellectual parlour games, but not for building educational systems.

d. ACADEMIC PRESSURES

Within the teaching profession, both at schools and universities, it is the argument from the increase in available knowledge that exerts much of the pressure to specialize. 'Knowledge pressure' seems to demand a narrowing of horizons. Some quite easy calculations based on Price's treatment of the exponential growth of science[22] can lead to some eye-opening—or at least mouth-opening—figures. For instance, it is not hard to get the result that 80 to 90 per cent of the scientists who ever lived are alive today; or to reach the conclusion that most of the papers ever published on a subject have been published since any of the

The Teaching of Science

teachers in that subject was born, or even since many of them qualified.

Clearly this is an important fact. I have insisted (section 2a) that cumulation and progress are salient features of the scientific scene. But before taking too seriously the consequences for education, it is worth pausing to ask how seriously we have to take them. Perhaps some statements have been too alarmist in tone, and we should not let ourselves be unduly daunted by a few percentages. Perhaps teachers are not, after all, going to be washed away by floods of new information, or blown sky-high by the information explosion. Or is this merely wishful thinking?

One relevant point is that it is hard to maintain that the amount of *significant* knowledge being produced varies directly as the number of people at work in the area, or the number of papers published in it. The proportionality seems likely to be a good deal less than direct[23].

Even if it were direct, there is still another point. Nobody has seriously suggested that what we have to teach, or should teach, is directly proportional to everything that is known, or even to everything significant that is known.

Medawar has even argued[24] that, in the life sciences, the factual content of courses is *lower* today than it used to be. He drives his point home by quoting from a zoology examination paper set in 1860, which is quite staggering by modern standards in the way it goes relentlessly on and on asking for one item of factual information after another.

The resolution of the paradox, and the explanation for apparent differences between various branches of science, are not far to seek. They are to be found in the different stages that theory has reached in the growth of its power to organize and unify facts. Physics has had a strong theoretical framework for centuries now, but the sophistication of that theory continues to increase—which helps to account for the feeling among senior physicists and engineers that many of the problems they had in their degree examinations would be considered not much above 'A' level standard now. Chemistry is in a rather different situation, having reached maturity rather more recently. At the teaching level, it has been considerably transformed even within the last few decades by theories of chemical binding and reaction

Specialization

mechanisms. Biology is in the process of undergoing an analogous change, with the rise of molecular and cell biology. Here, as in chemistry, there has been considerable scope for replacing the descriptive, 'natural history' approach and dealing less with particular examples and more with general principles.

Theory can do something then, to make the stockpile of facts manageable. It would nevertheless be very wrong for us to pin our hopes on it as an easy way out of the educational dilemma. For one thing, mastering more sophisticated theory does tend to make more strenuous intellectual demands on students. For another, particular facts remain the stuff of life and all-embracing theory can never replace them. One cannot help feeling a certain amount of sympathy with those who have grim forebodings of students who know a great deal about theories of covalent bond formation, but not the formula of methane. Stocking up with facts is not in itself the main purpose of education, but developing skill at coping with facts is of the very essence, and that cannot be done without facts to work on.

So—when the quibbling has to stop—there remains a genuine and substantial 'knowledge pressure' on teaching. There *is* more knowledge, and the people who have it burn with zeal to pass it on to the young. For the university lecturer who knows so much about statistical thermodynamics or transition metal complexes, and who spends much of his time increasing that knowledge, it is quite natural—all too natural—to be keen to share his information with others. Though the impulse is in itself entirely admirable, the blessings that flow from it are often mixed. The temptations of having captive audiences of near-virgin minds are strong, and the result is a tendency to pack more and more into lectures.

This means that the levels of attainment looked for in first degree examinations tend to be pushed up. And since the length of first degree courses in English universities is rather strictly limited to three (or in some cases four) years, there follows a tendency to demand higher levels of attainment at entry to the university. (To a first approximation it must, in the nature of the case, be levels of attainment rather than ability that go up, though it is difficult in practice to separate the two variables.) So the lines of strain extend backwards from university to school and force up levels of attainment at 'A' level[25].

The Teaching of Science

In theory, the boards that set 'A' level examinations should see 'fair play' between the demands of university departments and the realities of teaching and learning at school. These examining boards are heavily university-influenced (most bear the names of individual universities or groups of universities). Because of this, and because the demand for university places has undoubtedly acted as one of the main sources of pressure to specialize at school, one might wonder whether there is something to be said for leaving it all to the schools. Perhaps syndicates of schools instead of universities could be responsible for public examinations; or perhaps each school could examine its own pupils in its own ways and on its own syllabuses, with some system of external 'moderation' to achieve some kind of comparability of standards.

Such measures do not seem at all likely to solve the problems, and might well aggravate them. Opponents of specialization have, it is true, made universities the scapegoats, claiming that they have forced the system (its practice, if not its principles) on the schools—in effect, that schools are forced against their better judgments to perpetrate educational iniquities by wicked universities brandishing entrance requirements. Though the universities are certainly not blameless, this ignores the powerful contributory pressures that operate within the schools themselves. Teachers like advanced work for the prestige that it brings. Expertise confers status, and 'subject-mindedness' may be stronger among teachers than among their pupils.

The point that has some weight here is that, without their advanced work, schools could not attract and retain staff of high quality. This is another matter that depends largely on social attitudes and conventions, and is correspondingly intractable. It might help, though, to point out more forcefully that the schoolteacher who regards his school as a mini-university and tries to ape the methods of universities, apply their criteria and approach their standards of attainment is not likely to do a good job in the school environment. The dedicated schoolteacher achieves success, like anybody else, either by luck or by facing up to his own problems, not other people's. Schoolteaching has its own challenges and rewards. They bring to it its own dignity, so there is no need to envy or emulate the dignity of others.

In any case, how advanced need 'advanced work' really be?

SPECIALIZATION

What it often boils down to is the interesting bit of project work that one can open out into when one has 'got through the syllabus'. But one can, if one really wants, open out into interesting project work at almost any level of background knowledge. The level thought to be required is a matter of subjective judgment. University teachers commonly think that a student cannot do project work until he has ground through at least two years of university level facts and principles. But projects *are* done in schools even below the sixth forms. Surely the 'entry requirement' for project work is effort and time, not some absolute level of background knowledge.

Much of the academic discussion about the level of sixth form and undergraduate work really hinges around two related concepts which (like so many of the most important things) are difficult to pin down, dissect and describe. One is the question of the intellectual 'depth' which education is supposed to achieve if it is to be of high quality. The other is the question of the standard appropriate to a first degree, with the associated (though not identical) question of the level of attainment necessary to embark successfully on first research or first employment. Nothing much can be achieved without scrutinizing these two problems; so the next two sections are devoted to them[26].

e. THE MEANING OF DEPTH

The first and foremost point to make about depth in education is that no one seriously questions the value of it. Depth develops the mind so that it can see beyond the surface of things; it provides a meeting place where the minds of students and teachers can genuinely interact (with benefits that are far from one-sided). The emphasis on specialization in English schools (in so far as it is a deliberate policy rather than reluctant acquiescence to pressures) is an attempt to cash in on these admirable virtues. The real difficulty is not to know whether depth is a good thing or not, but to know what it consists of and how it can be achieved.

According to some, depth is a function of the intense concentration and focusing of attention that it takes really to master some subject area. The area must necessarily be small, but the student can acquire real familiarity with it and come to know

The Teaching of Science

his way about it—in short, he can 'get the hang of it'. He can appreciate its internal structure, its mode of thought and the direction in which it goes. The educational value of this, so the argument runs, is that a mind that has been trained by acquiring a real command over *something* — it makes little difference exactly what—can then apply itself later to whatever happens to crop up. This view has considerable merit (but see section 4g).

According to others, however, depth is to be thought of in a rather different way. They say that it means coming to see the subject in its setting and with its implications—developing an 'overview' (to use a transliteration of the German word) rather than 'tunnel vision'—and that it is this wider grasp which makes the difference between an honours degree and a high level certificate of proficiency for a laboratory technician. In other words, according to this second view, depth really implies breadth.

One thing about depth is obvious—it cannot be a presence-absence phenomenon but must be a matter of degree. It can vary all the way between the negligibly small and the unattainably great. No practicable teaching can go more than a fraction of the way up the scale. Anybody who claims to have dealt with a topic exhaustively in a course betrays himself as a half-baked scholar, with no conception of what serious scholarship really is.

Furthermore, it seems clear that the concepts of depth and breadth are not so much mutually exclusive as complementary when applied to intellectual matters. The words conjure up a simple geometrical model—knowledge as a volume that can be spread thinly over a wide area or sunk deeply down a narrow shaft; but this is inadequate and can be misleading. Depth is *not* synonymous with narrowness. It is all too easy to conceive of a three-year course that deals with nothing but chemistry, say, or botany, and yet fails to achieve any real measure of intellectual depth. This would be the case if it concentrated merely on 'multiple exemplification'—more compounds and their reactions, or more plants and their life-cycles.

Despite this, it is commonly supposed that the way to achieve depth is to study only one subject, or a small number of subjects; so it is worth asking just what a 'subject' really is. In the first place, how big is a subject? A little thought forces one to the conclusion that the way we carve up the realm of knowledge

Specialization

depends on decisions on our part which are at least to some extent arbitrary. Anybody who makes the effort to free his mind of the preconceptions that spring from existing subject boundaries and tries to imagine all human knowledge spread out before him must soon recognize that it just does not fall neatly into discrete packets. What Locke said is very applicable here: 'the boundaries of species, whereby men sort them, are made by men'. Is Chemistry a subject? Or Heterocyclic Organic Chemistry? Or Molecular Science, or Physical Science, or just Science? It is an illusion to suppose that we get any help from names here. A subject is as big or as small as we choose to make it[27].

Quite apart from size, there is also the question of the 'shapes' of subjects. The traditional ones are arbitrary not only in extent but also in the patterns of intellectual coherence on which they are based. However much we may be disposed by early upbringing to regard some patterns as 'natural', there are often alternatives which are equally valid and valuable. History, for instance, may be studied in periods, or it may follow certain ideas or activities or institutions through the centuries. (In caricature, one might study 'the period 1197 to 1199' or 'sex through the ages'.) In short, history may have either horizontal or vertical integration (to borrow terminology from the way in which the structure of industry is described). The study of living organisms, in a somewhat analogous way, may be divided into botany and zoology and then further subdivided according to the usual systematic classification; or it may adopt the molecular biology or cell biology approach, cutting right across the distinctions used for classification and looking at the whole range of living things (potentially at least) at the levels of organization of their molecules or their cells[28]. Each approach has its own type of coherence and its own virtues and limitations.

One type of intellectual coherence can be roughly described as looking at many things in one way. A number of traditional single-discipline subjects follow this type. But there is another type, which consists of looking at one thing in several ways. The classical example — it is literally 'classical' — is Greats at Oxford, which is largely a multidisciplinary study of the ancient civilizations[29]. The precise, 'hard' core is linguistic, and to it are added other aspects including the literary, historical and

The Teaching of Science

philosophical. Some of the courses of regional studies now available at a number of universities appear to be analogous in that there is again a basis which consists of the language of the region, supplemented by a study of its literature, thought, institutions and so on.

It is not impossible to construct formally similar patterns on the science side; in fact, it is on such a pattern that the Science Greats course at Manchester[30] is based. The precise core here is provided by physical science. To round it out and counterbalance it, there is the more open-ended treatment of science considered from the economic, social, historical and philosophical points of view.

New courses—whether at school or university level—normally mean new patterns of coherence. (The pattern may, of course, be more or less new, and the coherence more or less real.) Many of the recent ones claim to cross traditional barriers and relate what had formerly been kept in watertight compartments. Sceptical outsiders, however, are often left wondering whether they have enough 'depth'. The foregoing considerations give no pat answers to these claims and doubts, but they do at least provide a framework in which to analyze them.

The claims are often exaggerated. New courses (and the new institutions which spawn them so prolifically) commonly start with little intellectual capital other than novelty; so they can perhaps be forgiven for claiming more of it than they have. In a few cases they can even be recommended to have less than they claim, for novelty can degenerate into gimmickry. The evolution of the human mind has not kept pace with the recent progress of science; accordingly, emphasis on new intellectual relationships is likely to be at the expense of old ones.

On the other hand, some old course structures no longer represent the patterns of coherence that are most significant and most educationally valuable in the present states of the subject-matter and of society. Change does not take place as readily as it might in an ideal world, for educational inertia is great. It can be said of supporters of old course structures—as of supporters of old scientific theories—that the rearguard is never converted, it just dies off with the passage of time.

New courses should therefore be approached with a mind that is entirely open in both directions. There is no guarantee that

Specialization

they are better than old ones, and there should be no assumption that they are worse. There is no easy substitute for examining each case on its merits.

Most of the educational virtues (as distinct from the more clearly vocational ones) of what is called 'depth' really spring from the opportunities that the right kinds of coherence provide for doing certain things. These opportunities have little to do with whether the coherence is of the intradisciplinary or the interdisciplinary kind. Some of the more important of them are the possibilities for relating different parts of the subject-matter and for seeing problems and situations in more than one way; sometimes also for assessing conflicting evidence. It is by the scope for doing things like these that new course patterns are to be assessed for educational value—bearing in mind that it should really be the *students* who ought to exploit the opportunities. There is less value in them if only the teacher is in a position to do so. The knowledge and skills that students can reasonably be expected to have, and the sources of information that can be made readily accessible to them, must therefore be taken into account.

Novelty is a virtue in itself in one way. It can be very stimulating for a teacher who has taught a subject in its old shape for years. If he himself becomes fired with enthusiasm, there is a genuine benefit to his students, for enthusiasm is catching. But in so far as the effect is only one of novelty, it wanes as the novelty wanes. As far as the student is concerned, since he never knew the old way, he can hardly be expected to get excited over the novelty of the new one. Traditional and progressive syllabuses are all equally new to him.

f. Arbitrariness of First Degree Standards

As with ideas about subject boundaries, so with ideas about degree standards: it is hard to free oneself of preconceptions derived from the educational system as one went through it. The trouble is that the view one had as a student was a worm's eye view and, in addition, that memory plays tricks. In fact, the widespread idea that a degree standard is something that has to be maintained at a level fixed by some absolute criterion is largely an illusion. This is the conclusion to which one is forced when one examines the kinds of criteria that might appear to be applicable.

Degree standards cannot, of course, be formulated in terms of specific course material. The advance of knowledge and the growing sophistication of theory make it quite impossible in science. Even where it might be possible in arts subjects, it would be undesirable to insist on it because of the ossification that would almost inevitably result. The whole idea is so obviously wrong that it can be dismissed without further ado.

Perhaps one could say, instead, that a student should, by the time he graduates, be an expert in something. That sounds much more reasonable. Once again, however, trouble arises in interpretation and implementation.

It must be recognized, in the first place, that expertise (like depth) is a matter of degree. It is a mistake—potentially a serious mistake—to take as absolute what is really relative. There are precious few things that any newly-hatched graduate is properly qualified to do; and this applies even to the budding research worker, where the match between course content and job content is about as close as one can get. It is sometimes supposed that a first degree marks some definite watershed at which formal instruction can end and independent investigation can begin. This view is considerably oversimplified. An apprenticeship in research is a normal part of the training of a research worker, and the Ph.D., not the B.Sc., is the nearest thing we have to a licence to be a research scientist (see section 2c).

Further, the relation between first degree standard and the research front varies widely in different cases. In many of the more highly developed subject areas, course work at postgraduate level is already common, and it must and should increase. Less highly developed subject areas often afford easier opportunities for research-type work even at undergraduate level. The prospect of an early start on research is in itself an attraction for some students. Perhaps it is as well, all the same, not to go too far in meeting their quite understandable wishes in this direction. However attractive it may be in the short term to go helter-skelter for the research front on a narrow sector, it may not be in the student's best long-term interest if it leads to undue neglect of fundamental training on an adequately wide base.

In one way, research workers are *less* dependent on the specific

Specialization

contents of their undergraduate courses than other graduates, because they have the best opportunities and facilities for continuing to educate and re-educate themselves. This applies not only to research workers in universities but also to those in industrial or government laboratories, though here the match between course content and job content is in any case likely to be less close. But what of the graduate who goes into some job that is not primarily research?

The needs of industry are very varied, and no simple generalization can cover all cases. There is, however, quite a widespread feeling that a great deal of specialized expertise is often of little advantage and may in many cases even be a handicap to a graduate entering a firm (cf. sections 3g, 3h, 4b, 5b and 5j). Often the recruiting officers who come talent-scouting in the universities regard a degree only as a *qualifying* factor; they *select* by signs of adaptability and personality, and seem relatively indifferent to the splendour of academic achievements, whether higher or first degree, or whether honours or ordinary. As far as most types of employment go, specialized knowledge at entry is less important than a sound basic training coupled with receptiveness to a wide variety of factors outside the area of specialization — other scientific and technical factors, and also non-technical factors such as economic, commercial and political ones.

There is just one type of case where first degree standards bear a fairly definite relation to what the job requires—namely, where the graduate goes on to teach the subject he studied. Here it is standard that is relevant rather than specific content. It is felt that, in order to teach a subject effectively to a given level, it is normally necessary to have studied it to a rather higher level. Clearly this standard is an entirely internal one. It is self-set within education considered as a closed system.

With this exception, none of the criteria for first degree standards withstand scrutiny. Attempts to define them in absolute terms lose themselves in uncertainties or founder on inconsistencies. It cannot be done in terms of prospective job contents; nor are there adequate academic criteria of field of knowledge, or level of competence, or relation to the research front.

The meaning of this needs to be grasped fully. The point is not merely that selection of particular teaching material has to

The Teaching of Science

be to some extent arbitrary; over and above that, the criteria themselves elude definition—in so far as they have been considered so far.

There remains, however, one type of criterion that has not yet been mentioned. It may sound cynical, but it is actually idealistic. It is this: that the proper standard for a first degree is three years of hard, mind-stretching work by students of degree calibre. This standard is based primarily on considerations relating not to the contents of subjects, nor to the wishes of employers, but to the students themselves (cf. section 5a). A degree is the reward they get for three years' hard labour.

Many educators will recognize this fact when pressed, but in general there seems to be little conscious awareness of it. This is a pity, because failure to recognize it leads to educational mistakes and to stresses and strains which are neither necessary nor desirable. Much of the rest of this book is taken up with pursuing its implications. Chapter 5 examines the consequences it has both for the contents of courses and for the style of teaching. The rest of this chapter takes up two issues which, though different, are (as usual) related. They are the all-or-none attitudes which are prevalent in teaching, and the by now notorious swing away from science.

g. ALL-OR-NONE ATTITUDES

It is not difficult to see how the all-or-none attitude to teaching science arises. On the one hand there are the effects of cumulation, leading to a high intellectual entrance fee (section 2a) and the remoteness of the research front; on the other, there are restrictions due to academic conservatism and pressures about what constitutes proper first degree standards and therefore proper university level work. The effect is that young people are faced with what is uncomfortably close to an all-or-none choice as regards science. Either they go the whole hog to the intense specialization demanded by modern scientific research, or they have to rest content with all but nothing. Many of the ablest pupils in our schools give up science when barely in their teens[31]. To allow (and even encourage) this is to shirk a major problem that ought to be faced.

Not only scientific but also non-scientific specialization is

Specialization

responsible, of course. There is a popular myth that only science is specialized. Its popularity is quite amazing when one considers how easy it is to see that it is not true. The narrowest specialisms —and their most self-righteous defenders—are to be found in the arts, not the science faculties. This helps to account for an apparent paradox: despite the preoccupation with specialization in the English educational system, people are saying that it is amateurism which now deserves to be called 'the English vice'. The explanation is that so much specialization is non-vocational or even anti-vocational[32].

The theory of the mind well trained by having acquired a genuine command of *something* (irrespective of what that something is) has much to recommend it[33]. Unfortunately, science puts a serious limitation on it. There is a daunting 'numeracy barrier' to surmount. It is exceedingly difficult in practice just to pick up science, and especially physical science, starting virtually from scratch. Anyone can pick up a bit of history. (I am not suggesting that anyone can become a *good* historian, but only that anyone can become a historian of sorts.) With physics or chemistry, on the other hand, the problem is of a different order of magnitude.

Because of this, abandonment of scientific studies is in most cases a largely irreversible step, especially if not even mathematics is kept 'ticking over'. The converse situation — science students abandoning non-sciences—is not less serious but possibly less critical in that attempts to remedy it are not quite such forlorn hopes. There is not much of a 'barrier' to literacy. Nevertheless, many science and technology graduates are more deficient in this way than they should or need be.

The problems that arise out of all-or-none attitudes can be illustrated by considering the demands made by administration. Most graduates have to shoulder administrative responsibilities sooner or later in their careers, and this includes even those who remain primarily professional scientists as they attain seniority. It may be useful, however, in order to isolate the qualities required for good administration, to consider here in particular an archetypical case, namely, the administrative class of the British Civil Service—an administrative élite if ever there was one.

Administration is largely a 'generalist' activity. Specialists have in the past been distrusted because they were considered

The Teaching of Science

less likely to take the broad, unbiased view. This is one reason why most of our high-level administrators are arts-trained (not because arts courses are unspecialized but because they tend to specialize on 'irrelevant' areas). Administration, it is said, is 'done with the seat of the pants' and is a skill largely independent of the nature of the activity being administered. 'Administration is administration is administration', to adapt Gertrude Stein. But the limitations of generalists do make themselves felt. Scientific and technological considerations are increasingly coming to be components that are or should be intricately woven into decision-making processes (section 3i). Because of this, one might wonder whether it is good that the Civil Service has a rather low proportion of people with a scientific or technological background in the administrative class.

The selection procedure used for recruitment claims to be independent of the subject studied at university and to assess only general intellectual calibre. Yet arts graduates, and in particular historians and classicists, predominate among the entrants. The low proportion of science graduates can be partly explained by an obvious factor of motivation—most good science students want to continue with science beyond graduation. But that is not all there is to be said on the matter. There is an interesting point that emerges from an analysis by Dodd[34] of success ratios among those who do apply for entry. Success in the competition (the Method II open competition) correlates well with class of degree for historians and classicists, but badly for scientists. Among historians, there was one success for every 1·4 candidates with a first class, for every 4·8 with an upper second and for every 18 with a lower second; among classicists, the corresponding figures were 2·6, 5·0 and 31 but among scientists 3·4, 2·4 and 6·5. This suggests that the skills that administration calls for —at least in so far as they are identified by the selection procedure, which is a thorough and highly developed one—are not absent among science students but are less closely related to those which make for success in science courses than to those which lead to good performance in history or classics.

One may readily accept as a fact that the skills typically called for by science and by administration do not fully coincide, but that does not excuse what many consider one of the real weaknesses of our educational system. If students from

Specialization

traditional science courses have been able to develop the verbal dexterity and other skills basic to administration and related 'generalist' activities, it is as much despite as because of anything provided by their education beyond 'O' level. This need not be so, at least not to the extent that it is at present. There is no good reason why it should be necessary to renounce any substantial help in cultivating literacy as a price that has to be paid for scientific education. Conversely, the price of literacy need not be innumeracy[35].

h. THE OMINOUS SWING

The swing away from science has become a great talking point. Because of the widespread conviction that science leads to wealth (a conviction which is partially justified—see sections 3f to 3i), the prospect of fewer scientists arouses gloomy forebodings of poverty in nearly everybody, whether on the scale of the national balance of payments or on that of the family car.

The swing really is a striking phenomenon. Science subjects gained ground in schools steadily from the end of the Second World War until the late nineteen-fifties, when the trend reversed. The statistics no longer admit of doubt. Various debating points can be made about them, it is true. For instance, the decrease is in the proportion of science specialists among the sixth formers in England and Wales, not in the proportion of the whole age group (because more have been staying at school for sixth forms altogether). Then again, Britain already has a high proportion of university entrants in science and technology (45 per cent, compared to 35 per cent in the Netherlands, 32 per cent in France and 26 per cent in Western Germany), and this excludes substantial contributions from other forms of higher and further education. But, as the Dainton committee point out, the gravity of the situation lies 'in the deficiencies that will develop if present trends continue, rather than in the numerical consequences to date'[36].

No one can say precisely what the swing reflects, other than that it seems to be something quite deep-seated. It is at least amusing to note that 'the known start of the swing coincides chronologically with an upward trend in the illegitimacy rate and a marked increase in the juvenile crime rate. Are these all three manifestations of the same underlying state?'[37]

The Teaching of Science

Can the swing be against what is thought of (rightly or wrongly) as vocational specialization? The increase in sixth formers combining science and non-science subjects might support this[38]. But the swing does not seem to be confined to England and Wales, and is therefore not the result solely of the peculiarities of the educational system here. International comparisons are difficult because systems differ so much, but swings against science at university level have been observed in the Netherlands, Western Germany and Australia, though not in France[39].

This is puzzling, because nothing as obvious as Hiroshima and Nagasaki happened in the late nineteen-fifties or the early nineteen-sixties to change the public image of science[40]. Nevertheless, the public image does seem to be changing. It seems to be losing some of its power to fire the idealism of the young (which is still, of course, one of the great forces of the universe). It is as obvious to the younger generation as it is to their elders that the world we live in is very far from being the best of all possible worlds. They may have got the impression that science is too inhumanly materialistic and that it creates more problems than it solves; that natural science is already having too much effect, that the problems are social and that they should therefore study social, not natural science to set things right. If so, their idealism is at least partly misguided. The value of 'social' subjects for 'social' careers is sometimes overestimated[41]. If there were any truth in the picture of science as some kind of ferocious animal let loose and running amok in our midst, the best course might be to study not ourselves but the animal, so that we know better what it does and what it might do next.

Can the idea have got around that scientific careers are dull? This is possible. (Indeed, anything is possible here, given that channels of career information to schoolchildren are as tenuous as they are and that it would be difficult, even with a more generous allocation of resources, to make them really reliable.) 'Is science a bore?' asked an article in a national newspaper. 'At last people are daring to say it—scientific and technological studies fail to attract young people because they are largely boring and usually lead to boring occupations'[42]. Many young people would like to be 'managers'—sitting behind big desks and dictating to glamorous secretaries rather than working at the

Specialization

laboratory bench or walking round a plant in oily overalls. They may have the impression that it is easier to get to the right side of the big desk via arts or social studies than via science or technology; and, moreover, this impression has some foundation in things as they are, though not necessarily in things as they ought to be.

Can it be that the expansion of sixth forms has reached the limit of the pool of scientific and mathematical talent in the population—that all those with the ability that it takes to study mathematics and science with profit are already doing so? The Dainton committee satisfied itself that this is not so. What does seem to be the case, however, is that floating voters are drifting to the opposition. The evidence from drop-out rates—higher in arts than in science in England and Wales, the other way round in France—suggests an 'inertial bias' towards arts in this country[43]. The all-rounder who could do either more or less equally well is tending to opt for arts. Not committed either to D. H. Lawrence or to mathematical physics so deeply as to exclude the other, he is tending to choose D. H. Lawrence.

Possibly the most important factors are the ones most difficult to measure, like the quality of teachers and the inherent attractiveness of the course material as something to study. On the effect of teacher quality, the Dainton committee found no clearcut evidence and contented itself with a 'plausible but subjective opinion'[44]; but then, it is difficult to have anything other than subjective opinions when it comes to assessing personal magnetism. If many school pupils choose the most interesting teachers rather than the subjects currently reputed to have most value to society, they are to a large extent just showing the admirable good sense of the young. One cannot expect most of them to have the fate of the nation more at heart than their own, and it is to be regretted only that the two cannot be made to coincide more fully (which would mean, partly, ensuring that personal ambitions are formed against a reasonably realistic background of social requirements, since people are in general happier if they feel wanted than if they do not).

On the inherent interest of the material, there is no room at all for argument as to whether it is *potentially* there, but plenty of room for doubt as to whether syllabuses and teaching are right for making the potentialities actual. There has certainly been no

The Teaching of Science

lack of complaints in recent years, or of critical self-examination by science teachers. The issue is taken up in detail in the next chapter, but there is one point about the broad shape of careers that should be made here. The hour-glass shape (section 4b), narrowly constricted in the middle with a period of intense specialization, is not well adapted to increasing throughput. The lady may be inordinately proud of her wasp waist, but if she is not getting enough air, it might be a good idea to loosen the corset.

That is the sort of suggestion that is, indeed, being made. The swing has become one of the main arguments in the discussion about broadening sixth form curricula. The Dainton committee recommended that 'there should be a broad span of studies in the sixth forms of schools, and irreversible decisions for or against science, engineering and technology should be postponed as late as possible'; and that 'normally, all pupils should study mathematics until they leave school'[45]. Many educators, however, especially perhaps among the non-scientists, are much less keen to upset the existing system. It works very well for many non-science subjects, and they are naturally reluctant to acquiesce to what might be panic measures.

It is true that even among the scientists themselves there were few signs of discontent with the system as long as their share in it was increasing. They did not squeal until they began to feel the pinch. But this should not be allowed to obscure the potential gravity of the situation. In efforts to put the swing from science into its rightful place, it is sometimes compared to swings from other subjects—say the swing from theology since the middle ages—with the implication that everything must have its ups and downs. The swing from science is, however, specially serious for two reasons.

Firstly, it is serious because of the special relationship that exists between science and technology in education. The science-technology link, though complex and beset with uncertainties at the research level (section 3f), is solid and obvious and inescapable at the educational level. Top grade engineers and technologists come overwhelmingly from those who study science in sixth forms. Exceptions to this are not many in number (though they may be significant in quality).

Secondly, it is serious because of the essential irreversibility

Specialization

of the decision to leave science. Once somebody has decided to give it up, he rarely goes back to it seriously. The numeracy barrier is very selectively one-way—it lets people out but not in. Choices can be delayed by the educational system but not reversed once taken except in a small minority of cases[46].

There is, of course, human drop-out from science at all ages from the early teens upwards. That at school level is specially to be deplored because it is often based on choices which are particularly ill-informed and premature. To put the matter in an effective, if somewhat overdramatized way: it is carrying the cult of youth too far to leave the fate of the nation in the hands of 13-year-olds. But there is drop-out at higher levels too. Plenty of people who start as scientists move during the course of their careers into 'general management' in industry or into any of a wide variety of other occupations.

It is in these that many of them perform 'integrating functions' (section 3i); so this drop-out is rather different from that at school level. The people involved are often doing things that are important—filling a need which is possibly more urgent than that for more scientists to work in laboratories. It may be, if there is any truth in the analysis in chapter 3, that our most critical problem is not to get more people into white laboratory overalls, or to turn more of them more applied, but to key the activities of science (at the sort of level of manpower and expenditure at which we already have it) more effectively in with the other activities and aspirations of the community[47].

The very word 'drop-out' has disparaging connotations, and it is important to ask to what extent it is 'failed scientists' who apply themselves to integrating functions. To some extent, this must be so. In saying this, I certainly do not mean to imply that research is the only worthwhile career for a science graduate to follow for just as long as he can manage to avoid being thrown out of it. There are plenty of excellent positive reasons for a scientist to leave the laboratory behind him other than the negative one that he is not making a hit there. But failure is a relative matter, and one can fail at all levels of distinction. Possibly some of the Fellows of the Royal Society who leave their laboratories for greater or lesser parts of the time to walk the corridors of Whitehall and help to shape and guide the country's science policy would be less ready to do so if they felt themselves to be likely runners in the Nobel prize stakes. There is a quite natural tendency for those occupations which are the most direct continuations of education to retain those who are best in them. So it may be that the integrating functions do not get quite as generous a share as they deserve of top talents in their prime.

Much of the discussion about the swing seems to underestimate the importance of this. Scientific education has to fill this type of need just as much as the needs for organic chemists to synthesize potential drugs or aeronautical engineers to design the next generation of supersonic transports. The vacuum is filled at present partly by arts graduates, who often have the right kinds of aptitudes — the facility with words and with people, the mental agility to take synoptic views of the heterogeneous factors that bear on real-life situations, and so on; but they are often handicapped by a woeful lack of scientific background to take them even the first step or two across the numeracy barrier[48].

Perhaps it is here that the principal justification lies for pressure to continue mathematics and science on a broader basis at school. It is by no means certain that such pressure would in fact increase the number of specialists eventually emerging from higher education; the expectation is plausible but not free from risk[49]. We are on firmer ground in arguing the need to infuse more scientific background into the all-rounder group — not because they are the next best to the dedicated specialists but because they are the very best for the types of functions that we most need to strengthen. (The implications of this for reform are taken up in sections 5d to 5f).

i. A CASE FOR DIRIGISME?

'One of the characteristics of Britain is that 10,000 people will jump to the defence of academic freedom if they consider this to be in peril. Yet people talk about reforms which are only workable if they can be adopted uniformly'[50]. That is the uncomfortable dilemma raised by the interlocking issues of sixth form studies and university entry requirements and standards.

Education in England is permeated by an abhorrence of rigid centralized control, and with good justification. A teacher who is not encouraged to think for himself is less likely to encourage

Specialization

his pupils to do so. Rigidity kills enthusiasm, and the first prerequisite for communicating enthusiasm to the young is that the teacher should have some to communicate. Anxieties are therefore bound to be raised by the thought that reforming zeal, if frustrated at home, might cast envious eyes at more 'compact' systems in other countries[51]. There are many who would regard threats of centralization as more ominous than the swing. A remedy can be worse than the disease.

Nevertheless, there is a case for intervention from the centre when it becomes clear that the free play of the market is operating against the public interest. The signs are that sixth form specialization is an example of such a situation. There are arguments in favour of it, but some of them seem to be based on illusions and overall they seem to be outweighed by the arguments against. The persistence of specialization in its present form can be seen to owe a great deal to inertia and to pressures about which there is nothing specially desirable. Hence the temptation to plump for *dirigisme*. No one outside the centre can act effectively in isolation.

The Schools Council is central, but it has no teeth; its function is advisory and supervisory. Apart from it, there are three main parties in the situation—the universities, the examining boards and the schools. Within each of them there are signs of genuine desire for change but reluctance or inability to do so in practice, for mixtures of good and bad reasons.

The universities are reluctant to relax partly because many people in them take too restricted a view of their own functions; they tend to regard universities as guardians of scholarship only, and not as major social institutions as well. Such views show signs of being more firmly entrenched among junior grades of staff than among their seniors, a fact which appears paradoxical only until one remembers that it is the more senior people who have had more chance to come to appreciate the wider implications of their profession. There is also an additional reason for reluctance, which contains a more genuine paradox. The more enlightened and broad-minded things are often done by the institutions of relatively low prestige, well down in the academic pecking order of universities, and of departments within universities. Any apparent relaxation in the rigour of entry standards therefore runs the danger of being interpreted as a sign of weakness in competing for high-quality applicants, and hence of leading to a weakening of competitive position in reality. 'We are liberal about entry requirements' can come to mean, for too many people, 'our academic standards are low'.

The examining boards and the schools, whether reluctant or not, are unable to act except in concert. Neither is likely to make a major success of a less specialized option while a more specialized one is available. The schools could not put their best pupils into them because it would mean cutting them off from high-prestige universities, since it is so difficult in practice to avoid confusing ability with attainment. There is also the pressure from highly qualified schoolteachers to exercise their own specialisms, which perhaps does not take sufficient account of their less highly qualified colleagues or of the fact that schools are not well placed to cope with change and progress in knowledge (a source of real difficulty even to university teachers, who have better opportunities and easier facilities for dealing with it).

So who will cut the Gordian knot? We have *dirigisme* already on educational issues that are at least as controversial, though that in itself is no argument, of course, for extending it. Perhaps *dirigisme* is rather too strong a word for what is really called for. It might be that all that is necessary is to add pressure to persuasion. Some of those most reluctant to act alone might be (or soon become) those most grateful if reforms were adopted with some degree of uniformity[52].

CHAPTER FIVE

REFORM

a. CRITERIA FOR CONSTRUCTING COURSES

When one comes to look at ways in which better courses might be constructed, the biggest difficulty arises right at the start, because there is no simple criterion to apply. The various factors that have to be balanced are not only heterogeneous but incommensurable—that is, they are not only different in kind but they lack any workable common measure. In the absence of a common measure, it is necessary to rely on judgment to balance them. This is a job which educators have to take on. If there is anything that makes an educator more than just a teacher, surely it is the attention he pays to this sort of thing. Taken seriously, it is a tough responsibility, but one he should not shirk. No one else has comparably direct contact with all the main factors that bear (or should bear) on the situation, and for that reason any form of 'consumer research' that might be undertaken among students or among potential employers has to be taken as a useful source of evidence but not of ready-made and ready-to-use recommendations.

What, then, should the educator bear in mind? Perhaps philanthropy deserves (by virtue of its nobility) to be given pride of place among the aims of education. There *are* teachers who are fired with the ambition to make the world a better place. Contact with the young may help to keep that spark alive where it would otherwise have died. A cynic might well be right in saying that nations get roughly the educational systems they deserve; but it is still proper for educators to want to make them deserve better educational systems than they have. However, the effects of education work themselves out slowly and it may be better, even in the long run, to concentrate on more immediate objectives. Accordingly, educators are probably well advised to focus their attentions on the things with which they have most direct contact. The proper spirit for them to cultivate is one of philanthropy clearly recognized to be vicarious.

The more immediately relevant factors to consider fall into three broad classes—those relating to the subject, to the students and to their prospective careers, respectively.

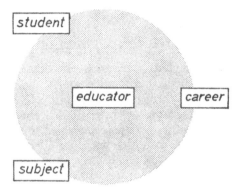

So the ideal educator, the paragon of all the educational virtues, combines an easy mastery of his subject with a profound understanding of his students and a keen awareness of their career prospects. He has to arrive at some kind of synoptic view of all these in deciding what and how to teach.

As so often, the factors are all mixed up with each other in a tangled skein. Of course there is a sense in which every one of them is concerned with helping students. Nevertheless, the distinctions are useful for structuring a discussion because they point to genuine and realistic differences in emphasis. It is quite possible to take the view, for instance, that students can be helped best by concentrating on the subject, or alternatively by giving pride of place to career considerations. Thus one can distinguish subject-oriented, career-oriented and student-oriented approaches to the problem.

The first of these—the attitude that attaches prime importance to subject considerations in constructing courses — has really been dealt with already in the preceding chapter. It amounts to the view that the best thing to do is to push a student's knowledge of a subject as far as possible—that is, to specialize in it.

Reform

To put it in a nutshell, specialization is a subject-oriented teaching mode.

Society should, of course, have an interest in preserving and fostering the well-being of subjects, and universities are the institutions principally responsible for doing it. They are guardians of scholarship, and it is their duty to advance the interests of subjects by perpetuating knowledge of them, keeping it alive and increasing it. But as far as undergraduate teaching (or any course work) is concerned, it is really rather naïve to suppose that the interests of a given subject are automatically best served by exposing as many students as possible to it for as much of their time as can be managed. The 'greatest knowledge of the greatest number' is not necessarily the best way to ensure progress in a subject.

The pressure for specialization in university teaching derives largely from specialization in academic research, which helps to account for the extent to which specialization is non-vocational (see section 4g). It is not hard to see what it could lead to if allowed to develop to excess. That way lies the ivory tower—and not just one ivory tower at that, but a profusion of separate ones scattered through the university. The danger, as far as teaching is concerned, is that specialization is adopted as a teaching mode not because, after due consideration, the conclusion is reached that it is the best thing for students, but because university teachers are too blinkered by their own research interests to want to do anything else[1].

b. RELEVANCE TO CAREERS

When taxed on the question of the relevance of their courses to prospective careers, university teachers commonly expostulate with some indignation that they are *educating* their students, not *training* them for jobs. There is a good deal of righteousness in this indignation. What lies behind it does, of course, include some narrow-mindedness masquerading as concern for academic freedom, but there are also some more worthy considerations.

The issue really boils down to this — that the fit between education and career is rarely close and often barely detectable. This is a matter not just of present practice but of largely unalterable principle. With the best will and skill in the world, education cannot achieve anything more than a very imperfect match with what careers demand or with what employers think they demand. Job contents are too many, too varied and too unpredictable, and to a greater or lesser extent they are unteachable anyway[2].

Nevertheless, it is an important fact about science courses that they do have vocational relevance. In pre-medical and engineering courses, the relevance is quite obvious and marked, in most other cases less so, but in no case is it absent (even if one excludes the particular career possibility of teaching, which could make any subject vocationally relevant). Out of this fact spring the arguments—which are and should be endless—about the conflicting claims of purity and applications, of science and technology, of technology and technical management and even of technical management and general management.

The views of employers are obviously important here and should probably be taken more into account in universities, though with appropriate pinches of salt, because employers (like other people) are not always themselves in the best position to see clearly what is good for them. They need experts even to help them to formulate their requirements, the experts in this case being educators. Employers are sometimes short-sighted or misguided, and they tend to exaggerate the directness of the relation between means and ends, as is natural among those who are amateurs in the field of education. It is best, therefore, to accept their statements as relevant information but not as detailed specifications for the shape and content of education or as final judgments on its success.

In considering the relation between education and career success, facts are scarce, but comment is free[3]. It is one of the things that even hard-headed industrialists are prepared to give for the asking. Most of the points of substance in it can perhaps be taken under three main heads — issues of personality, of excessive purity and of management unawareness.

Personality, or quality of character, is something that employers look for in recruiting just as much as brains, and often more so (see section 4f). Career success in industry and elsewhere depends on energy, dynamism, drive and toughness just as much as on intellectual ability. It is often said that this is the reason why career potential cannot be measured by examination per-

Reform

formance, but this is not entirely true; examinations are partly tests of achievement and therefore measure other qualities in addition to ability[4]. Such qualities are therefore not neutral in education. Nevertheless, there is plenty of room for argument about the extent to which it is possible for educators to do anything drastic to shape personality and attitudes, and consequently about the extent to which they ought to try (except in a negative sense—there is clearly something irresponsible about actively motivating students against the qualities that make captains of industry).

Excessive purity, both as regards knowledge and as regards attitudes, is a frequent source of complaints from industrialists. Recently recruited graduates are said to be deficient in awareness of the real problems of industry, and in real desire to apply their information and skills to solving them.

The attitude factor is a natural—if not necessarily inevitable or desirable—consequence of the tendency of students to mirror their teachers. A university lecturer cannot, in the nature of the case, be a full-blooded industrial scientist as well, though there is certainly room in Britain for a good deal more sharing and interchange of personnel than takes place at present.

Purity in attitude is certainly regrettable to the extent that it reflects not lack of inherent interest in industrial problems but sheer ignorance of them. There is a story which is at least symptomatic and is said to be true as well. A certain firm takes good care to recruit a few top-notch science graduates every year by offering them a lavishly equipped laboratory and freedom to do what they like. Once the bright young men are settled in, a crisis is artificially 'rigged' on the production line and they are approached in apparent distress. Could they please leave their research for just a few days to help sort out the mess? Many of the young scientists get so interested in the real-life problems involved that they are at last weaned from pure research.

The question of excessive purity in knowledge is of a different type. Enlightened employers want flexibility in their recruits rather than ready-to-use tailor-made products because they recognize that topicality in scientific and technological education—early attention to current views and procedures — can easily become a matter of more haste, less speed. Basic topics are considered to be basic partly because they are applicable to a variety of practical situations. To be taught 'how it is done' can become a barrier to thinking about 'how it might be done better'. Accordingly, if education is to avoid excessive rigidification in the minds of the young, it must leave introduction to industrial practices largely to industry itself. The educational system could not, in any case, tailor-make courses for all functions in all industries for the simple reason that there are too many of them. Both on the grounds of flexibility and of feasibility, therefore, much of the responsibility must be taken by employers. Industrialists have, in fact, thought seriously about the matter[5].

Take, as an example to illustrate the issues involved, a hypothetical but not unrealistic proposal to institute a course of studies at a university in 'X science' or 'X technology', where X is some product for which there is a substantial demand. The proposal is made with the admirable intention of increasing the usefulness of the university to society and the course must, of course, be called an honours degree course so that it attracts applicants of high quality. The argument against the proposal is *not* that the subject-matter would be intellectually unworthy. There are doubtless plenty of worthwhile problems in the field of the X industry where demands on knowledge, intelligence and ingenuity are genuinely challenging and where new answers could make real improvements in the product or the mode of manufacture. But it is this very fact—the prospect of technological progress — which holds the danger. Change marches inexorably on; some new process may make existing ones obsolete or a new product Y may oust X altogether. Then the prospects for scientists in the X industry are dim and they are left with an injured feeling that society has failed them.

Against this, the argument *for* the proposal is that contact with applications of science is good for students. Which particular applications are chosen does not matter much, but *some* applications are better than aloof purity. Courses of the 'X science' type are commonly composed largely of basic mathematics and physical science, with no more than a generous flavouring of X. As such, they might be quite a good form of preparation for careers in industries apparently not at all closely related to X. Indeed, they might facilitate the 'technology transfer' from which important advances often come[6]. Thus the overall merits and demerits of the proposal depend more on the details of the

Reform

educational approach than on what appears in the title of the course.

Complaints by employers that graduates are not sufficiently aware of management considerations are, similarly, only partly realistic. Admittedly, graduates need not be taken quite so completely by surprise as they sometimes are (according to boardroom stories) by the fact that commercial considerations do intrude on the operations of scientists in industry; but again, there are severe limitations on the extent to which the relevant things can or should be taught.

Engineering courses are naturally more aware on this front than the purer science courses. The whole issue is tied up with the question of what constitutes 'management potential' and the extent to which technical jobs are a route not only to technical management but further across an ill-defined boundary into general management.

If industrialists' views on the qualities of managers were used uncritically to construct an 'ideal' education to produce them, one would probably arrive at some kind of mixture of accounting and operations research, with subsidiary courses on golf and alcoholic drinks (practical work included, of course). Educators may readily accept that the skills implied by this are indeed important in industry but may feel, nevertheless, that it is not the right kind of intellectual diet for good quality minds in their late teens (not as a main constituent, anyway). There *are* things about management that can be taught—the concept of Business Schools is founded on that—but management, like administration, is largely an art done 'with the seat of the pants'[7]. To that extent, managers are born rather than made. Management potential can therefore emerge from almost any kind of academic background.

It is rather dangerous to put too much faith in the idea that a young man who has devoted his studies to 'management' is all set to be a brilliant success at managing anything there is to manage. Hence the philosophy of the two national Business Schools is that, for those destined to go to the top, management principles as such are more properly a postgraduate than an undergraduate study—not necessarily to be taken immediately after graduation, even, but just as profitably as 'post-experience' work after a few years in industry. This seems the right way to greater professionalism in management, and it leaves the way clear for easier and more frequent transitions from technical jobs to management (see section 5i).

c. A STUDENT-ORIENTED APPROACH

Having now noted that the subject-oriented and career-oriented approaches have their limitations as well as their virtues. it remains to look at the third possibility suggested by the diagram in section 5a—namely, student-orientation. This is complicated in itself because, clearly, subjects and careers are considered at least in part and at least in intention with the benefit of students in mind.

By student-orientation I do not mean necessarily doing what students want or think they want. The very complexity of the factors to be balanced means that they are not in the best position to judge; they are rather worse placed than employers, though the deficiencies are different in kind. The responsibility for shaping education lies fairly and squarely on the shoulders of the educators. If I argue here that what we need in present circumstances is a shift in emphasis towards student-orientation, what I really mean is that the needs of students should to a greater extent form the pivot around which the educator balances other considerations.

This may sound suspiciously obvious. It may appear to say merely that education is really for the sake of students, which is an empty platitude. But it is not entirely empty really. Consider the case of the lecturer who, near the end of his allotted number of lecture periods, gallops through facts and comes out of the lecture theatre flushed and slightly breathless, saying 'I don't suppose they took much in, but I had to get through it'. Why did he feel he had to get through it? Because of a sense of duty to his subject—a feeling that some set standard in it ought to be reached. If that standard is really arbitrary (section 4f), then he was driving himself and his students for the sake of an illusion.

Or consider the people who argue that one must fit this and that and the other into the course of studies somewhere because the students will need to know about all those things when they get out into the world. This sometimes shows an overdeveloped sensitivity to outside needs. All the pressures from various types of possible careers come into play, and the result is a cluttered, inflated and bitty teaching programme.

Busy and highly qualified people *do* spend a good deal of time arguing about what should go into courses, at staff meetings in university departments and at examining board meetings to frame or revise syllabuses for school examinations, and much of the argument *is* conducted along subject or career lines. With the number of pressures that operate, it is little wonder that the results are often not as streamlined as they might be. (One is reminded of the saying that a camel is a horse designed by a committee.) They way out of such an impasse, surely, is to recognize one type of consideration as overriding. If the paramount place is given to the interests of students, then the educator must keep at the forefront of his mind that he is teaching students rather than subjects, and for their own sakes first and those of their future employers second. He has to think not how much of a subject he can get through, or how far he can meet the wishes of employers, but what and how much his students should be given so as to do them most good.

There is one thing that the subject and career lines of argument have in common. Both concentrate on *what* is to be taught. The result is that there is a built-in tendency for syllabuses to become overloaded, with all the effects that has on *how* they are taught. As is widely recognized, cluttered syllabuses exert a baneful influence on the quality and the style of science teaching.

Yet, if considerations relating to subjects and careers could be kept firmly in place *behind* those relating to students, it would become clear that it is the *style* of teaching that is the most vital thing about it. Student-oriented teaching must concentrate not on what the course covers but on what it does to students; that is, it must attend less to what is taught than to how it is taught. If that could be effectively achieved, the clutter would almost automatically drop out. A student-oriented overloaded teaching programme is a contradiction in terms. If it is successfully student-oriented, it cannot be overloaded.

d. STYLE, NOT CONTENTS

The things that are so often wrong about the style of science teaching are mostly connected with the idea that science is

The Teaching of Science

tantamount to nature-story (sections 2c and 2d). Teaching becomes too factual. Lecturers think that the right thing to do when they stand in front of their audiences is to give them facts about nature.

Now it is true, of course, that there are a great many facts in science. There is no getting around it, and students should begin (but not finish) the process of stocking up with them at school and university. Science courses cannot be all fun and games and 'discussing'. (As the saying has it, one cannot have only currants in a cake.) Nor is it a bad thing that there should be plenty of facts in courses. Skill at coping with facts is the real mark of a well-trained mind, and it cannot be developed without facts to work on (section 4d).

But there is no reason why a lecturer should have to give all the facts by word of mouth. There is an unwritten but widely accepted convention that the 'content' of a university science course is what the lecturer puts into his lectures. Hence course work for science students tends to consist largely (apart from practical work—see section 5f below) of taking and learning lecture notes. There is much frantic scribbling in the lecture theatre, followed by evenings spent deciphering the results and committing them to memory. Studying science becomes stenography[8] plus memorization. The result is that numbing of the mind with facts that is all too familiar to many people.

A common reason for preferring non-science subjects is that they often give more scope for a range of reading, with opportunities to think about the material and discuss it. There is, of course, a very genuine educational value in this. Bacon's advice on reading—to taste widely as well as chewing and digesting a few books thoroughly (section 3e)—was admirable. The ability to read not only intensively but also extensively, yet selectively and critically, is an important one for education to cultivate, and the most effective way to do so is to call on students to deploy facts and arguments from the reading matter either in writing or orally[9]. Most students like doing this sort of thing anyway. It gives their minds the exhilaration of exercise, and they feel themselves 'being done good to'.

It is worth considering, therefore, how far it might be possible and desirable to move in that direction in the teaching of science subjects as well. Subject-matter does not, after all, impose its own

Reform

unique teaching style, and there is consequently no need to accept fatalistically that things must continue to be taught in the way they have been in the past. There seems to be no reason in principle why science teaching should not put more emphasis on reading books and articles and less on listening to lectures and learning lecture notes. Facts can be got from the printed as well as the spoken word. If students get many of them by private reading, then teaching time and effort can be spared from merely presenting material for discussing it, elaborating on it and talking round it. The feeling that 'there just isn't time' to do these things derives from the view that lectures must 'cover the ground' and must therefore be fact-laden. Time could be made by relying rather more than is now customary in science departments on well-selected reading lists.

This line of thought clearly has rather far-reaching implications, and I would like to follow them up in more detail here. A reading list should indicate clearly a core of really basic material. This should be of realistic dimensions; strict moderation is called for in deciding what it should cover[10]. There could, on the other hand, be any amount of supplementary reading. In other words, the reading list should have a firm and clearly defined base but be open-ended upwards. The supplementary reading (given, of course, with indications of the nature of each item to help to guide choices) could go in various directions according to what seems appropriate in different cases. It could contain more advanced facts and theories, but it would be good in many cases to think seriously about other possibilities as well. There is a good deal to be said for branching out into selected practical applications or social implications rather than pushing straight ahead with more 'textbook stuff'.

The potential importance of the reading list core is this. One of the villains of the piece in university science teaching is the lecturer who is too clever by half. Intent on proving his originality, he gives a brilliant set of lectures that is quite different from anything to be found in the books. His students are duly convinced that he is not the inferior kind of teacher who 'teaches from the book'; but they are also left stranded in nearly total dependence on their lecture notes. It is difficult for them to read the material for themselves, however willing they might be to do so.

The Teaching of Science

There is a real danger in this, not to be dismissed with a wave of the hand and an airy remark to the effect that it is good for a student to get more than one view. So it is, but that does not solve some of the difficulties that arise. The selection of material by an individual lecturer may verge on the idiosyncratic, going beyond the point where the personal approach pays—in the inclusion of particular classes of compounds or particular metabolic reactions, for instance. Or, where a rather difficult proof or derivation is involved, there may be different symbols or conventions in addition to a different approach, which can be quite unnecessarily confusing to a beginner.

Keeping down the size of the core is important in order to leave some apparent 'slack' in the teaching programme. Useful advice to someone planning a course might be this. Think of a reasonable amount of material to go into the allotted number of teaching periods; reduce that amount by 10 or 20 or 30 per cent (according to what seems appropriate in the circumstances); and then exercise iron self-discipline to keep to the new limit, because that, in many ways, is where the real education starts. Better underload than overload. No educator yet has solved the problem of the quart and the pint pot, and so apparent slack is necessary to leave room for students to take supplementary as well as core reading seriously and to think, possibly talk and even better write about it.

In this kind of way one might effectively answer the Dainton Report's call[11] for more 'breadth and humanity' in science teaching. 'Humanity' does not mean just occasional pieces of outside reading such as Koestler's *The Sleepwalkers* or Watson's *The Double Helix*[12] which show that scientists can be just as peculiar people as non-scientists. More genuine and sustained breadth and humanity can come from an approach which calls on students to do things more active than listening and memorizing; and from the way in which broader reading can be made to grow at all levels (not just at the end) out of the course material, with the opportunities this gives for the minds of students and teachers to meet on common prepared ground[13].

Educationally, it makes admirable sense to throw students back on reliance on their own reading to a considerable extent[14]. It should develop their ability, willingness and confidence to tackle any subject on their own—virtues which are supposed (in

Reform

popular mythology, at least) to be the strong points of arts graduates. Indeed, the style of teaching I have outlined is altogether more like the traditional arts style than what is usual in science.

By virtue of this, could it perhaps be a way of countering the swing away from science (section 4h)? Perhaps some of the most effective ways to increase the attractiveness of science are to be found by concentrating not on the contents of courses but on the style in which they are taught. If (and to the extent that) there is a problem of catching the 'floating voter' between scientific and non-scientific studies, the best policy may be to emphasize the similarities, not the differences. (As in politics, a shift towards the centre *could* work both ways, but the most likely outcome is to increase the catchment.)

It seems at least a possibility, and the point is taken up again in each of the next two sections. In the meantime, it may be worth while briefly to recapitulate some of the main points that bear on this issue, separating what will be widely regarded as fairly obviously true or desirable from the suggestions for achieving the desiderata.

It is hardly open to debate, in the first place, that an education that neglects science is not likely to be the best way to fit most people for life in the last quarter of the twentieth century. Nor, in the second place, will there be many who deny that young people opt against science because, as usually taught at present, it lacks certain attractions (which are partly genuine educational advantages) that other subjects have or appear to have. Most people will share my confidence that science courses (or at least science-based courses) *can* be devised and taught so as to have the major educational virtues concerned.

One of the main suggestions is that the difficulties that stand in the way stem largely from ideas about levels of attainment in subjects, often reinforced by a partly subconscious residuum of the view that the real purpose of science teaching is to produce scientific specialists (in a way markedly different from the teaching of, say, history or classics, which does not similarly assume that the production of anything other than professional historians or classicists is merely some kind of secondary fall-out).

The way to catch floating voters, it is further suggested, may be to concentrate on adjusting the style rather than the contents

The Teaching of Science

of science teaching. Success depends only partly on finding and including easily discussable topics. There are plenty of topics (like drugs or abortion) which anyone can discuss and where views are all too readily forthcoming. The main point of education, however, should not be to score easy successes in getting discussions going, but to provide practice in using sources of facts, in treating them in ways that are at least selective and where possible critical, and in marshalling the facts to present and assess situations. A good deal of this can be done with material that is in or not far removed from the standard contents of science courses.

Throwing the emphasis on reading matter makes it possible to do these things without some totally unrealistic staff-student ratio. It enables students to work effectively on their own, developing the kinds of skill likely to be useful in later life. Not many graduates are employed to take lecture notes and learn them, but most are expected to be able to read things up.

e. THE FORM OF SYLLABUSES

The last section had universities most in mind. It is time now to look at the corresponding issues in the school environment.

Here there is one objection that might easily be raised and can as easily be answered. Some people might say that, although it could work very well to leave relatively mature university students more to their own devices, the same could not be done with pupils at school. But there is really no substance in this objection, given goodwill and common sense. Primary school pupils have been known to be set homework that involves reading up a topic. If ten-year-olds can do it, why should sixth formers not be able to?

The main contrast between the university and the school situations is a quite different one. It lies in the fact that course contents are not primarily in the control of the teachers themselves. So it is the examining boards that should exercise restraint on their behalf in keeping down the contents of facts and theories in the syllabuses they set. Those who frame the syllabuses should apply some modern educationist's version of Occam's razor, to the effect that 'items must not be unnecessarily multiplied'; which might be paraphrased, 'if in doubt, leave it out'.

Reform

There is another point about syllabuses, rather subtler than the matter of their sheer volume. It concerns the form they take —the way they are written down. If one looks at an 'A' level science syllabus, one finds a list of facts and principles about nature. It is almost enough in itself to prove my point about the way that science is taken to be tantamount to nature-story (section 2c). Many arts syllabuses, on the other hand, have a very different look about them. One often finds lists of books or documents. Arts sixth formers are clearly expected to read. Why not throw out equally broad hints to science sixth formers?

This need not mean an arbitrary choice of one or two textbooks out of the many available, selected as set books for a few years. The proper comparison is not with English literature, for a novel or a poem is a highly individual piece of writing to be studied in itself, not for what it describes. Science is more like history. History happened in only one way, to just the same extent that nature only exists in one way, but there are many different ways of writing about it. Thus history syllabuses are sometimes given not as long lists of historical facts but as short lists of books which give an indication of the scope of the subject, with hints that candidates may be given opportunities to show their acquaintance with these books. Alternatively lists of historical facts (which correspond to the nature-story facts of science) may be supplemented by 'prescribed documents' which illustrate and highlight important items.

This way of putting syllabuses gives a clear lead to teachers not only on content but also on style. Sixth formers are pushed into reading books and documents, and teachers are pushed into discussing them instead of reciting facts. It would not be impossible to go at least some way in this direction in science syllabuses too. There is, after all, no shortage of interesting books and articles that are relevant and easily available.

The implications of this line of thought go beyond the classroom. They include not only the question whether science is a dull subject but also the question whether science teachers are dull people, and whether this might help to turn school pupils away from science subjects. The Dainton committee found that, as far as formal qualifications go, science teachers compare not unfavourably with teachers in other subjects[15]. Yet there is a widespread impression that they are less stimulating as personalities. Headmasters say (in private) that they cannot in good conscience put pressure on their pupils to go into the science sixth when it is not hard to see that there are more 'live wires' among the teachers on the arts side.

Can it really be true that scientists are dull? Somehow it seems immensely unlikely that there should be any inherent dullness about them. The subject-matter they have studied is potentially as interesting and exciting as any there is to be studied. But it is true that they may not be used to bringing that interest and excitement out in words. They are used to learning facts and grasping difficult concepts rather than talking and writing about them. Science teachers were largely taught that way themselves, and syllabuses reinforce educational inertia to push them into teaching their pupils that way in turn.

It is all too obvious that there are inherent characteristics of the subject-matter that are responsible for this. Nevertheless, there is plenty of stuff that can be found in it or made to arise out of it that is eminently suitable for talking about. Present syllabuses provide no help or encouragement to do so, which is a pity, since it would give teachers a chance to show themselves as well as their subjects in a more interesting and attractive light. Moreover, it would have a corresponding educational value for pupils by helping them to develop fluency with verbal ideas, which is an aspect of maturing into interesting personalities. It is what a person has to say that makes him interesting.

There is no need here to go to excess and adopt a stereotyped caricature of the scientist as some inarticulate social outcast with nothing to say for himself. The facts are often very different. Not all scientists are 'poor value' as dinner guests. There are plenty of chemists who are ebullient, and conversely, there are plenty of historians who are dull. But if there were no bias in the opposite direction, it would be despite and not because of what education does for them.

f. IS PRACTICAL WORK OVERRATED?

In the considerable movement that has taken place during the nineteen-sixties to infuse new life and vigour into the teaching of science at school level—not paralleled by anything of comparable scope at university level where, in the nature of the case,

Reform

initiatives are more isolated—much faith has been put in the 'investigational method'. The idea of getting pupils to find out more or less for themselves is not, of course, new in itself; it was embodied in the 'heuristic method' for teaching chemistry which Professor H. E. Armstrong was advocating around the turn of the century[16]. But there has been a renewed emphasis on using the principle in recent years. It has become part of the current conventional wisdom—or at least the conventional idealism—of educational thinking.

Before the principle can be embodied in practice, a question of interpretation arises. Finding out is all very well—but how? One learns by doing, agreed—but doing what? Activity is the only road to knowledge—but what kind of activity?

It is a mistake to suppose that the laboratory is the only place to find out (cf. section 2d). The current faith in practical work of the investigational type is not exactly misplaced but quite possibly exaggerated. Such work is not the long-sought panacea; nor is it the only alternative to the dull routine of memorizing factual information.

Schoolteachers themselves get very keen on new approaches—which in itself is half the battle won—but their enthusiasm is not untinged with scepticism about the value of pupils finding out for themselves in the laboratory. This is not only because of the demands it makes on time and on money. Both of these *can* be found if there is a good case. Demands on time mean fewer facts—that is, a lower syllabus content; and that is a price which, in present circumstances, we can afford to go on paying for some time yet as long as we get the right kind of return in the form of minds which are lively and inquiring and not going under in a morass of information.

The case for investigational work in the laboratory rests partly on its supposed resemblance to the 'real thing', creativity in research, and the hope that in consequence it will stimulate and foster the right kind of abilities and ways of thought. Essentially, it is a kind of simulation technique for training research workers. In practice, however, reservations have to be made about its efficacy for that purpose, quite apart from the validity of the purpose itself.

Firstly, pupils normally find out just what the teacher wanted them to find out—nothing more and nothing different. They get out of the work just as much and just as little as the teacher builds into it. There is nothing wrong in this, of course—it would be astonishing if it were otherwise—but it is as well to be clear and explicit about the limitations and not to overestimate the value of simulated creativity by underestimating the role that guidance plays in it.

Secondly, and more serious, there seems to be some misconception about the real nature of the scientific process. Practising scientists do not get all or even most of their information in the laboratory. To suppose that they do ignores the requirements of cumulation. In order to stand effectively on the shoulders of their predecessors and to be able to see further (section 2a), they must find out most of what they know by reading books and journals and by listening and talking to other people. The use of the lecture theatre and the seminar room and, more especially, the library is therefore at least as important as that of the laboratory.

Teaching and studying outside the laboratory should, accordingly, be done not just as a concession to inadequacies of time and money. Practical work would not be the unique ideal method in any case, because other skills, notably skills in acquiring and processing information from reading matter, also have to be developed. Perhaps printed matter is currently the most under-utilized teaching aid in presenting science, and there could with advantage be some shift in emphasis from test tubes and Bunsen burners to books and articles, and from filter paper to writing paper. Pupils can, after all, find out for themselves by reading as well as by experimenting, especially, perhaps, as they get older and more mature.

The proper role of well-chosen laboratory work is to act more as a focus of interest than as a major source of knowledge. As such, demonstrations may be even more effective than do-it-yourself work at the bench. There is greater scope, and pupils do not get hung up on technical details about glassware and stoppers and so on which can be more exasperating than educational.

Of course, technical details are not trivial to practising scientists[17]. A chemist does have to learn how to use a pipette properly, and that efficiency of stirring may very easily make the difference between success and failure. But—and this is the really important point—scientific education is not and should not be only for future practising scientists. Science is too impor-

Reform

tant to be left to the specialists, and therefore scientific education must attract and cater for a wider range of talent—in type, not necessarily quality—than the totally dedicated boffins.

Here there emerges another aspect of the attempts towards a 're-unification of culture'. In the educational context, they surely call for more emphasis on cultivating the image of scientists as well-read scholars, not as 'rude mechanicals' who are always getting themselves dirty in the laboratory. To say this does not at all imply accepting the Platonic kind of intellectual snobbery, trying to make science into an activity for ladies and gentlemen kept at a very decent distance from the money and the muck. The actual effect may well be the opposite of this. Courses that lean heavily on practical investigation are usually (despite protestations to the contrary) weak on useful applications, as they are on other wider implications of the basic material. It is perhaps inevitable that they should be. There is not much scope for investigating industrial processes or social side-effects or philosophical consequences in the school laboratory.

The question of practical work raises another issue which is quite closely related, though it applies, perhaps, more particularly to the university than the school environment. A moderate amount of 'active underemployment' is good for young people. It allows them to develop their own interests, to engage in extra-curricular activities and to mature as personalities. As is well known, arts undergraduates tends to be better off in this respect[18]. Long hours spent chained to the laboratory bench can be very inhibiting[19].

g. INTEGRATION OF SUBJECT-MATTER

Everyone agrees that integration of subject-matter is a good thing. In this respect, it is rather like depth (section 4e)—indeed, the two issues are clearly related, though they are not identical. Here again, however, there is more than one way to achieve the aim, and so it is necessary to look carefully at it before pushing ahead towards what it seems to be. Moreover, it is appropriate to ask how overriding the importance of integration really is in constructing courses. If I argue here that its importance is not paramount, that it is not the sovereign remedy for curing educational ills, I do not wish to imply that it can safely be ignored. I mean to point out only that it does not by itself guarantee success and that it would therefore be a mistake to pin too many hopes on it, because attention would thereby be diverted from other factors which may be equally or more crucial.

I have discussed previously (section 4e) the fact that patterns of integration are not uniquely determined by the subject-matter. Many valid ones can be found and used, and some of the possibilities for coherence are really quite subtle. This means that, although they may be present in the mind of the teacher at the beginning of the course, they are not likely to dawn on the students in any significant sense till near the end of the course (if at all).

Take, as an example to illustrate the questions that arise, the proposals that have been made to replace sixth form physics and chemistry by a single subject, physical science[20]. Much of the discussion centres around the extent to which the subject-matter can be integrated and around the advantages that might be gained from such integration. It is not difficult to draw diagrams showing how all the main topics are derived from one or two key concepts—matter and energy, say—with a lot of lines showing the total interconnectedness of everything with nearly everything else. Exercises of this kind are certainly interesting and possibly even valuable for teachers, but how much they help students is debatable. Some of the connections are rather artificial, and in any case teaching cannot be done according to such schemes, since time has one dimension less than a block diagram. A teaching scheme must take the form of a linear sequence, although cross-connections can and should be indicated at points along its course and diagrams are obviously valuable for tying them together.

When it comes to the crunch, there is no getting around the fact that there are topics which just do not integrate readily. Structural isomerism just is not closely and significantly related from the student's point of view to moving coil galvanometers. But then, neither is it to the effects of temperature and pressure on a gas, which occur with it in existing chemistry syllabuses; nor are any of these bound up in any intimate way that beginners can grasp with the general properties of oxides or with radioactivity. Similarly, with biology syllabuses. Although the existence of relationships is not difficult to see, a little cool

Reform

scepticism is not entirely out of place in considering how close the intellectual interdependence really is between floral mechanisms, the cranial nerves of dogfish, catalysis by enzymes, Mendelian inheritance and the properties of soils. The same could be said of surface tension, ferromagnetic properties and formulae for thin lenses in physics syllabuses.

The principal argument in favour of a physical science subject depends not on integration of subject-matter but on the fact that, by giving one subject title where there were formerly two and correspondingly reducing the amount of material covered, room would be made for sixth formers to do more other things as well. It is mainly by the desirability or otherwise of that change that the scheme must stand or fall.

A measure of variety in subject-matter is not something that needs to be apologized for, and hidden as far as possible by straining the meanings of words. There is a certain amount of delusion (both self-delusion and the other kind) in connection with subject titles. It arises partly from the idea (deriving from superficial views about what makes for depth) that young people must be given the illusion, if not the reality, of studying only one thing. Neither for the reality nor for the illusion is the necessity beyond question. Life is varied, so why should variety be taboo in preparing for it? Many students like doing more than one thing; they want to avoid the feeling that they are circus animals being trained to do only one kind of trick.

Some confusion and misdirection of effort arises from the use of the same word 'integration' in two different types of context. One is internal integration in the subject-matter; the other is integration of the subject-matter at its boundaries with other branches of science and also with non-scientific considerations. (It is the latter sense to which section 3i refers). Too much attention to the one is liable to lead to neglect of the other. Limitations of time and of human mental abilities mean that only a limited number of integrations can be achieved in any course. Some choice is therefore demanded—not an all-or-none choice, but a matter of emphasis between two different kinds of integration, the inward-looking and the outward-looking.

The danger of not paying enough attention to integration of subject-matter, or of interpreting 'integration' too loosely, is that superficiality may result. There are, however, other sources of superficiality, and some of them may be more important than lack of proper integration. One of them is excessive striving for up-to-dateness, and this is examined in the next section.

h. UP-TO-DATENESS

Up-to-dateness is certainly good for motivation. Undoubtedly it generates enthusiasm in students if one can give them the impression that they are being taken right up to the front line where it is all happening, for reasons rather similar to those which make a live broadcast more popular than a recorded one. In other ways, however, up-to-dateness is a mixed blessing. It can make good presentation and integration more difficult, and it can slide into superficiality.

It is true, needless to say, that 'historical accretions' do tend to stick to syllabuses over the years, and jettisoning these may meet more resistance than it should in an ideal world. Teachers have a natural tendency to want to teach most of what they learned themselves *plus* the new additions to knowledge; indeed, this is one of the main pressures that make for overloading. It is genuinely difficult to reassess something that one was brought up to think of as basic. But there are also honest and valid differences of opinion, and it will always remain partly a matter for judgment what is *avant-garde* and what is stick-in-the-mud. So hints to put the brakes on keeping up-to-date should not without further ado be written off as mere sops to the conservatism of the teaching profession. There can be more behind them than sheer inertial reluctance to change.

At university level, the attempt to take all last year's research papers into account when giving this year's lectures springs from the most admirable motives, but it can become a Sisyphean task[21]. It can absorb effort which might be better devoted to other things. In areas where the rate of change is small, it makes little difference. Where the rate of change is great, a cynic might well say that two-year-old errors make just as good teaching material as those only one year old, and both will be almost equally dated by next year, when the students might want to use the knowledge for something other than passing examinations. Budding research workers are most susceptible to such obsolescence, but at the same time they are also best placed to update their undergraduate work; scientists not in research work are more likely to use old knowledge than new (section 3g). As far as lecturers themselves are concerned, many feel that they teach the material best about the third time round; by then they are not yet stale but know the difficulties. Over-frequent drastic revisions may tend to lower teaching standards.

At school level, it is even more important to face the fact that the realities of the teaching front are not the same as those of the research front. To keep really up-to-date is not only a Sisyphean task but impossible and potentially confusing as well. Even with all the in-service courses in the world, schoolteachers are not well placed to keep up with a rapidly moving and fluid research front. They might do well to remember that teaching material does not always lose its interest and value as it ages.

As sources of news from the research front, certain glossy semi-popular scientific magazines find much favour. Some of them do indeed set a very high standard. Nevertheless, excessive reliance on them carries its own penalties. Sixth formers fed with them can sometimes ask what appear to be the most penetrating questions on controversial research-front topics; but they cannot even begin to appreciate answers that match the apparent penetration of the question. They want merely a glib conclusion as to whether the answer is this or that—a mere nature-story answer—and are in no position to understand even in outline on what basis the answer is believed to be this or that. The apparently penetrating question, in fact, is really quite superficial.

There is nothing wrong with this kind of knowledge as long as it is recognized for what it is—just 'general knowledge'. Everybody's knowledge of most things is of this type. It could not conceivably be otherwise. But the spearhead of a sound education should be different. It must be built on some firmer intellectual discipline than the shifting sands of bare conclusions. It cannot always be based on strict reasoning and conclusive evidence, but its items of information must contain relations—if not to evidence then to something else, such as other items of information or possible experiments or uses or wider implications. Otherwise there is nothing there but the sheer superficiality of isolated facts.

Keeping up-to-date in this kind of way is sometimes referred to as 'toeing the party line', and there is more in this wry

The Teaching of Science

humour than might appear at first sight. Bare facts from the research front stand in the same kind of relation to a real education in science as do this year's pronouncements from party headquarters to a real education in politics. It is an advantage, naturally, if there is more than one party, because that helps to make people ask what is *behind* the pronouncement.

i. LIBERALIZING SCIENCE COURSES

In general, the standard of teaching science subjects in British universities is really quite high. Obviously it is variable, and obviously there are plenty of faults that one can find with it (section 5d), but by and large the staff are competent and enthusiastic. They enjoy relatively low average teaching loads and are often taunted by outsiders with being more interested in research; but considering that their promotion prospects depend overwhelmingly on research output (despite some half-hearted official protestations to the contrary), the devotion most of them show to undergraduates is quite touching.

The main criticism to be levelled against them as regards the contents rather than the style of their courses is that they are often too restrictive in outlook. They consider their functions to be confined to science *per se* in a rather strict and narrow sense. There is a certain amount of an inbreeding mentality about them.

Understandably, applied departments tend to be less afflicted in this way. Quite apart from considering applications of their subject-matter in industry, which is after all part of their function even in a narrow sense, they are increasingly including other material designed to help graduates find their feet in the industrial environment. Courses on aspects of economics, management techniques and law quite often fit under the umbrella of engineering syllabuses.

This reflects the fact that broad-minded engineers think of themselves as performing integrating functions (section 3i). The definition of the engineer as 'the creator of projects of engineering significance'[22] is symptomatic. Engineers are seen as planners and co-ordinators who call on the specialist services of technologists and applied scientists and integrate them with all the other things that have to be—or at least should be—taken into consideration in building a power station or producing a new type of car.

Reform

The implication here is that the engineer becomes much more than a specialist himself and turns into a high-level manager. There is certainly a lot to be said for this route to top management. It is more common in other countries with successful records in science-based and technology-based industry (section 2f), and accordingly firms here have been urged to adopt it more freely.

The trouble is that engineering courses still have not met with all the success they potentially deserve in giving the right public image of themselves. To a large extent, managers are born and not made (section 5b), and the young man with management potential is often not prepared to put up with the immediate prospect of a few years' calculations on the bending of beams and suchlike for the sake of the more distant prospect of a post with a rich blend of technological with human and other interests. It is rather like offering young men their pick of the most beautiful girls in the world on condition that they promise not to see any girls at all for the next six years. The response is bound to be limited. Modern heroes are not like those of mediaeval romances, and notions of renunciation do not fire the idealism of large sections of the population.

Science courses too—even if not overtly applied—can and have been 'liberalized' by adding other matter, to the extent of anything from a dash to a half. In the technological universities (the former colleges of advanced technology), a substantial timetable allocation for general studies is the rule; even in traditional prestige universities quite high up the academic pecking order, options of the kind are no longer unknown; and in new universities (those founded from scratch since the Second World War, starting with Keele) it is quite common to find patterns of study that range freely across the traditional divisions not only between departments but also between faculties. In all types of university, joint honours courses have proliferated. While the majority of them confine themselves substantially within single faculties, a fair number span broader ranges. For instance, courses of study combining some kind of engineering in more or less equal partnership with some kind of economics or management studies are offered by quite a substantial number of universities, under a rather confusing variety of names.

The output of graduates from such courses raises the question of 'scientific generalists'. This term has acquired a certain amount of currency but no precise and agreed meaning. In a correspondingly vague way, it is assumed that the people so described will be specially well fitted for various integrating functions (section 3i).

It seems that two distinct types of concept are included under the name 'scientific generalist' — the multispecialist and the science-oriented humanist. The multispecialist acquires more than one area of specialization, often all within science and technology. This can, of course, be highly fruitful (sections 2e, 4b). Important contributions have been made by physicists or chemists moving into an area of the life sciences; a person who knows both about control engineering and about some process technology might be useful in automating the process.

Science-oriented humanists are in principle quite different. The concept derives from Sir Leon Bagrit's Reith Lectures in 1964, where it was used to mean broadly trained, adaptable people destined to become leaders in politics, industry, commerce, the trade unions and in particular the Civil Service. To fit them for such key positions, Bagrit suggested that they should be given a 'university course combining the humanities with some of the sciences'. They would have 'some understanding of science, its history and philosophy, and of the direction in which science is moving', but would not really be scientists or technologists. 'I do not want the world to be run by scientists and technologists, because science and technology are of value only as servants to society. I want to see at the head of affairs basically educated men, science-orientated humanists. They must understand the values of mankind, they must have a view of history and a view of the future. They should have a strong flavour of science and technology about them, but not enough to turn them into scientists'[24].

If this kind of ideal could be effectively translated from an industrialist's vision into an educational reality, the products would presumably be as well qualified as an education could make them to fill the roles of D. K. Price's 'middlemen' (section 3i). They should have scientific awareness rather than expertise; be able to understand experts rather than be experts; and be in a position to ask many of the right questions without, of course, being able to answer most of them.

Reform

How effectively can joint honours courses combining science and humanities meet these ambitious specifications? Fairly well, in some cases. Some combinations are good. But many others are not distinguished by any real sense of purpose, either educational or vocational. In a way, it is all too easy for a university to set up a joint honours school merely by putting together halves of two existing honours schools[25]. The danger of overloading becomes even greater than for single-subject honours courses. It is recognized that many combined courses are tough on students, and employers, for their part, show no great enthusiasm in most cases. In general, therefore, and with exceptions, joint honours courses are at once taxing and unattractive.

An alternative and perhaps more acceptable (though more difficult) solution is to devise courses where breadth is achieved not by juxtaposing two more or less independent and possibly disparate halves but by attempting to integrate topics in new ways into teaching material that meets some criterion of depth (section 4e). There is no unique optimum solution to this problem — it is of the sort which clearly calls for initiatives by individual universities.

There is one group of topics which deserves special consideration in this context—that which is becoming known (though not altogether happily) as the 'science of science'. The title is meant to imply that science becomes an object of enquiry in itself, something to be looked at and studied by the concepts and techniques of other disciplines, with the purpose of reaching a better understanding of what science is, how it behaves, what effects it has and how it can be managed. Thus it includes the history and philosophy of science, pursuits which are well known and already used in universities on a limited but slowly expanding scale: and also the economics and sociology of science, now important as some kind of basis for science policy[26]. Educationally, this group of topics has, over and above the general 'arts' virtues (opportunities for wide reading, open-ended discussion and extended written work with scope for independent thought), two more particular virtues. Firstly, it offers some degree of intellectual coherence with the rest of the science course (coherence by what is looked at, of course, rather than by how it is looked at—that is, the multi-disciplinary kind of coherence of section 4e). Secondly, the subject-matter itself is of more direct relevance to the sort of integrating functions to which (according to the argument of section 3i) science students should be prepared to apply themselves (see the Foreword).

Similar considerations apply to the choice of topics where only a dash of liberal matter is to be added to a course which remains predominantly scientific or technological. The broad alternatives are freedom or coherence—either range of choice or integration of subject-matter. One cannot in general have both. In education, too, one cannot have one's cake and eat it.

On the one hand, one can aim at coherence and use topics of the science of science type as adjuncts to the main scientific or technological studies. On the other hand, one can also settle for contrast and offer a wide variety of topics chosen from the whole range of human interests. Some students like to be able to take something totally unrelated to the main bulk of their work—modern English drama or Greek civilization or Renaissance painting. They find the contrast refreshing. However, it becomes difficult to meet any criterion of depth. There is a danger, too, that students come to rely on little 'mini-courses' for snippets of information. If what is wanted is a smattering of knowledge about the industrial revolution or the Great Depression, then surely it is better to cultivate the tradition that a student takes two or three books away for the week-end.

The matter of coherence applies to the selection of teachers as well as topics. There are some real advantages in *not* calling in outside experts on history or economics or drama. Visiting lecturers can, of course, be good, but they can also all too easily be a waste of time. In the extreme case, some august personage drops in, delivers his pearls of wisdom to the assembled audience and then departs. If he is really august, the pearls would probably have been readily available as books or broadcasts anyway. The students are left after the lecture with nothing much more than they could have got by watching one of the better current affairs programmes on television.

These criticisms need not apply, of course, if the teaching is done by staff from other departments of the same institution. But one could also go further and make more effort to get it done by the staff of the 'home' department. In that case, it could be given real relevance to the main body of studies. There is, of course, an obvious objection: the staff do not know about 'outside' topics. Perhaps, though, one should not too readily take no for an answer here. A little pushing would probably reveal that they know more than might have been imagined. Even in the most humdrum department, the interests of members of staff do spill over into the wider implications of their subject. Further, since the staff remain on the spot, there is at least plenty of opportunity for follow-up discussions and even for written work that can be criticized. Again the objection is obvious: many members of staff cannot write good essays themselves. And again, it may be as well not to be unduly daunted by the objection. In many cases, it is probably unfounded; gifted but semi-illiterate scientists do exist, but they are rare. Even if it were well-founded, it would still not matter so very much. The important thing is to get the student to write a piece of extended prose on something that interests him, in the knowledge that it will be critically discussed by someone else who is also interested in the topic.

The educational effect of such exercises would be mutual. Having overcome their initial inhibitions and put in the necessary activation energy, many members of staff would probably come to enjoy them, finding themselves stimulated to broaden their own horizons. The inbreeding mentality is a matter of attitude rather than of coverage. The effect on staff-student relations might be salutary, too. At last something would be provided that can be discussed by research worker and undergraduate on a footing approaching equality! Plenty of members of staff would be glad to discuss but cannot get going in a tutorial because they cannot find the right kind of topic. On the one hand they naturally do not want to descend to the trivial, and on the other hand there is little scope when dealing only with scientific facts or theories that students cannot remember or grasp.

j. POSTGRADUATE COURSES

The supervision of research students falls beyond the scope of the central theme of this book, but this must not be taken to mean that it can be sharply separated from the teaching function. Quite on the contrary, it is a vital aspect of it. To produce people with master's and doctor's degrees is just as much a part of a university's teaching function as to turn out B.A.s and

B.Sc.s (cf. sections 2c, 4f). Distinctions between the demands of teaching and research seem often to be made in considerable ignorance of the realities of the situation. If there are conflicting claims on the time, energy and interests of university staff, they are not so much between teaching and research as between undergraduate teaching and postgraduate teaching.

There is a rule of thumb, now in fairly common use, according to which a science research student is counted as equivalent to three undergraduates in assessing teaching loads. This gives the feeling and the flavour of the situation somewhat more realistically. The demands of research supervision are not measured merely by the number of hours actually spent with individual research students (even if coffee-times are included, as they should be). The value of taking a research degree depends largely on being pitchforked into a laboratory where lively and successful work is going on. A research student learns how to solve problems by seeing problems solved around him. Hence a flourishing research school is necessary for proper performance of the teaching function[27].

All this has to be set against a certain amount of criticism now current that the Ph.D. degree is being misused and that the system is getting a little out of hand. The Swann Report[28] brought evidence that the attractions of higher education and academic research might be depriving industry and schoolteaching of too many graduates, especially good ones. The point is not just that entry to professions outside the universities is delayed by a few years; rather, it is the fear that Ph.D. work in universities may tend to engender ways of thought and attitudes which are of little use or even inimical to success in those professions and may make it more difficult as well as less attractive for people to enter them[29].

At its worst, Ph.D. work may not be good even by internal academic standards. It sometimes looks all too much like creeping along the frontiers of knowledge with a magnifying glass, looking for something to do—though, to be fair, that is probably more common in faculties other than those of science and technology. In science, the situation is usually not that problems are difficult to find but that they crop up all too easily and automatically. The research process has its own built-in self-perpetuating momentum (section 2c). Once a line of research

REFORM

gets started, it can become quite difficult to stop it. The question asked is often of the form, 'is it worth doing more work along this line?', and to that the answer is almost inevitably yes—there is always more to be found out. But it might be better to ask, 'which of the many possible lines of research is most worth doing now?' The implications of that question can be too disruptive for comfort, and so the point is rarely pushed to the stage of action. Research workers themselves are not immune from the dangers of becoming trams instead of buses.

It is worth bearing in mind also that the prestige and promotion prospects of an academic depend largely on his continuing to produce research papers with his name on them, and these normally include papers on what is done by those working under him. There is such a thing as empire-building within the academic world.

In considering postgraduate work it would be a mistake, however, to think only of research. There are things other than research that it is quite possible and proper for graduates to stay at the university to do. The growth of course work at postgraduate level has been marked in recent years and there seems to be a good case for encouraging it to continue, both in the form of some attendance at lectures and classes by candidates for research degrees and in the form of degrees and diplomas given mainly for course work. The latter alternative means that those for whom a fourth year of university study is in some way justified can be given the chance of having it without making it a standard prescription for all[30]. Furthermore, the mere existence of postgraduate courses helps to relieve artificial pressures on the contents of first degree courses. It means that the ideal of bringing students to the frontiers of knowledge before graduation (section 4f) can be seen to be unnecessary as well as illusory.

It need not and should not be supposed that the only valid purpose of postgraduate courses is to deepen primary specialization. Given that most first degree courses are more or less narrow straitjackets, there is a good case for some people to spend an extra year or two of study on something different. This need not mean encouraging a young man to hop from department to department, taking one first year course after another while he postpones still further taking any decision about his career. Nobody wants the eternal undergraduate, and there is the 'argument from physiological ageing' against letting the type proliferate. Young people sometimes need to be gently pushed into growing up instead of developing Peter Pan complexes.

Bearing this in mind, there still remain some worthwhile reasons for making a more or less fresh start either immediately after graduation or a few years later as 'post-experience' education[31]. Among these reasons the following are distinguishable, though not absolutely distinct. There is the need to provide for a change in emphasis—for instance, for a chemist to go into one of the more chemical kinds of biochemistry. Then there is the need—which differs from the first only in degree and not in kind—to acquire a new area of specialization. This might be in another area of science or technology, to create a multispecialist (section 5i), or it might go further afield, for instance to a Business School. Finally, there is the need to round out certain aspects of education which might have received inadequate attention, whether through necessity or neglect, at the first degree stage. This could, for instance, give a chance to graduates from rigorous scientific disciplines to cultivate habits of extensive rather than intensive reading and to develop skills of writing extended prose (sections 3e and 5d) in subject areas appropriate to their ages and interests. With the concomitant widening of horizons, this would produce as an end result something rather like the science-oriented humanist (section 5i).

Thus it seems important at the postgraduate as well as at the undergraduate stage not to be too hidebound by traditions. One should be guided by potential value to students, not by arbitrary ideas about subjects that impose constraints on what can be considered to be a proper level for postgraduate work. Teaching material and reading matter are not necessarily inappropriate for 21-year-olds just because they might also be comprehensible by 18-year-olds. To suppose that they are would very effectively force postgraduates to behave as trams instead of buses.

k. SCIENCE FOR NON-SCIENCE STUDENTS

Science for non-science students means providing some sort of contact with science for students after they have decided to devote their main studies to non-science subjects, however soon that decision takes effect or however long it is delayed. It is an

Reform

activity which is relatively neglected—much more so than the converse attempt to bring something of the humanities and social sciences to students of science and technology. The two can to some extent fruitfully be made to overlap, but the one is usually a good deal less effective than the other. 'General Studies' in sixth forms are commonly more successful with arts than with science topics (section 4a). In universities (leaving aside the marginal case of the relatively infrequent interfaculty joint honours courses—cf. section 5i), science courses for non-science students are almost non-existent except for some brave tries in new universities.

The difficulties are formidable, it is true, because of the high intellectual 'entrance fee' (section 2a). Rather obviously, the more background the students can be taken to have—the longer the decision against science could be deferred — the easier it becomes to do something worth while.

Many experts find it difficult to hit the right level for laymen without obviously 'talking down' to them in a patronizing way. They have so much background themselves—there is such a lot that they have come, through constant use, to take very much for granted—that it is not easy for them to identify what will prove to be stumbling blocks[32]. Even those who are willing and able find themselves discouraged by the prospect of disparaging comments from their professional colleagues in their own subjects—'oversimplified', 'woolly', 'lacks rigour', 'there's more to it than that', or even the scathing 'journalistic'. This can be a serious drawback of public lectures, and as a matter of practical university politics there might be something to be said for arranging sessions *in camera*, where experts would find it easier to let their hair down.

There is a clear analysis by Yudkin[33] of various forms that can be taken by science courses for students whose main studies are not scientific. Of necessity, it is based largely on American experience. Four main types are considered.

The first is the 'introductory course'. This is used where it is not possible to provide a special course for non-scientists, so that they have to take the same course as those who intend to go on to further studies in the field. Its weakness is that it is designed as the foundation of a large building and 'cannot satisfactorily be made to serve as a complete bungalow'.

The Teaching of Science

The second type is the 'general survey course'. This type is common in American universities and accounts for much of the suspicion in Britain of American 'general education'. It has the advantage that it is clearly understood to be terminal and not introductory to further study in the subject. However, it is accused of superficiality in treatment and of encouraging an uncritical attitude towards study. Further, it suffers from the 'Gradgrind Fallacy'. 'To learn what facts have been discovered about the observable world is not to study science.' (This corresponds closely to the Fallacy of Misplaced Concreteness of section 2c and to my diagnosis of the main factor in spreading it. The almost inevitable consequence of trying to cover too much science in a course is to present it as just a mass of 'nature-story' facts.)

The third type is the 'course in scientific method', which purports to reveal the method by which science progresses. The trouble with this is that there is no agreement on how this method is to be described and in what terms it should be analyzed[34]. Many of the current versions are obviously unrealistic (and can, indeed, do more harm than good, as I have tried to show in section 2b).

The fourth type is the 'case histories course'. The most notable example of this is the kind proposed by Conant, which has enjoyed some popularity at Harvard and elsewhere[35]. Conant made it quite clear that by 'understanding science' he did not mean being well informed about the facts and principles of science, but rather having some kind of 'feel' for the 'tactics and strategy' of science. He suggested that this can be got from detailed study of case histories drawn from the early phases of scientific disciplines.

Yudkin criticizes this approach on the basis that written accounts inevitably give scientific work the appearance of a mechanical and routine activity, and that the role of the reader becomes passive[36]. These criticisms are not, however, necessarily valid. It depends on what type of printed accounts are available and how they are treated.

Conant's vision has, I think, a great deal of value in it and is in most respects educationally sound. He has a good point, for instance, in suggesting very limited historical episodes. History of science is no educational elixir that is effective however it is

Reform

presented. It has been said that a few lectures on the history of science are 'the provincial Vice-Chancellor's answer to the two cultures problem'. This is a much unkinder cut than the facts warrant, but the note of cynicism is not groundless. It reflects the fact that history of science can be just as dull, stale and unprofitable as any other subject. The main danger, as always, lies in trying to cover too much. The course that scampers through from the Greeks to Darwin, giving just the main events and dates, is of little more value to a student than learning the dates of the kings of England. It is when a situation is studied in more detail, so that students begin to see the complications and the interplay of varied kinds of factors, that the educational returns become more than to scale with the time and effort invested. So there is a great deal to be said for severely limiting the time-base of the course and extending 'coverage' in the direction of fuller discussion of the implications of events rather than increasing the number of events.

Conant points out that, in the early stages of sciences, it is possible to study the scientific process without a great deal of scientific knowledge as background, which makes the approach suitable for laymen. The big question that naturally arises is whether the process is the same in advanced science as it was in early science. Obviously it is different in some ways, but there are still important respects in which the fundamental similarities outweigh the differences.

A perceptive point made by Conant is that the strength of the professional tradition in which a scientist now works makes it almost automatic for him to be to a high degree impartial, objective and accurate while he is inside the laboratory. This puts modern science at something of a disadvantage as a means of educating people to apply whatever may be good and appropriate in scientific methodology to social and human problems (cf. section 3e). The early stages of natural sciences, by contrast, were confused and often more polemical than reasoned. Methodologically, therefore, they correspond better to the present state of some branches of enquiry into human societies and behaviour, and they may accordingly be a better source of object-lessons about how to approach them.

In two respects, Conant's approach seems unnecessarily limited. In the first place, there is no good reason why historical case studies should not be used with science as well as with non-science students. They represent *par excellence* the kind of broadening topic that is different from but still related to their main studies (section 5i). With science students, one can meaningfully discuss the question of the differences between early and modern science. One could also combine science and non-science students in a class; few other kinds of topic give comparable opportunities for bringing them together with something approaching parity of status, for each might have genuine but complementary contributions to make to discussion.

In the second place, case histories need not concentrate only the 'tactics and strategy' of science itself. They are not necessarily confined to internal considerations of how science advances but could also illuminate its external relations and social implications[37]. In sections 3b and 3c I have sketched very briefly some sample treatments of this kind.

In fact, history of science need not be 'pure' history. It can be made a springboard for discussing science from various points of view. Historical events can lead into aspects of the philosophy of science, discussed in a literary way rather than in the style of formal logic. They can also lead, through discussion of social implications, to an introduction to some of the issues of the sociology of science[38].

This whole group of topics is much the same as the 'science of science' type of material which can be used to 'liberalize' science courses (section 5i). When such topics are adapted for use with non-science students, they do not, it is true, provide a real substitute for science proper, and to some extent it is shirking rather than facing the issue to let them stand proxy for science in education. They make a very imperfect 'science surrogate'. But they may well be better than nothing. They do give some feeling of contact and familiarity with science and its ways. And they do this without demanding a prohibitive entrance fee in the way of mathematical preparation or background of scientific nomenclature, facts and principles. Chapters 2 and 3 of this book contain samples of topics of this kind, and the bibliographies for those chapters could serve as a start for reading lists.

NOTES AND REFERENCES

Chapter One

1. 'Processes of teaching and learning carry out a function exactly analogous to that of biological heredity, in that they serve to specify the character of the new generation. This similarity in result can be indicated by referring to this method of passing on information as "socio-genetic" transmission. The development of what is in effect a new method of heredity must inevitably lead to the appearance of a corresponding new method of evolution.' (C. H. Waddington, *The Nature of Life*, Allen and Unwin, 1961, p. 110.)

2. They do tend, of course, to get inflated by a little honest self-interest on the part of academics. 'There is nothing an ageing professor likes better than a little civilized windbaggery about the aims and purposes of his humble career: the transmission of wisdom, the discipline of freedom, the formation of man: Rousseau, Bacon, Newman, Arnold ... virtuous fudge, not least because one feels a brute to attack it' (F. Hope, 'Are Arts Graduates Employable?', *New Statesman*, March 22, 1968).

Chapter Two

1. J. B. Conant, *On Understanding Science*, New American Library, 1951, p. 34. Conant's treatment may be compared with that of J. M. Ziman, who sees the essential difference between science and non-science in 'the sort of consensus of free and well-informed scholars that we ordinarily find in the Natural Sciences' (*Public Knowledge*, Cambridge University Press, 1968, p. 19). In such subjects as history, philosophy and politics, 'to stick to ascertainable public "facts" is to limit the discourse to the banal' (p. 26). Consensus is clearly an element in the establishment of the research traditions which make cumulation possible. As I emphasize in section 2b, science does not stick to public facts either; the point is that it achieves a greater degree of consensus about general principles.

2. T. S. Kuhn, *The Structure of Scientific Revolutions*, Chicago University Press, Phoenix edition, 1964, pp. 19-21.

3. M. Polanyi, *The Study of Man*, Routledge and Kegan Paul, 1959.

4. G. K. Chesterton, *All Things Considered*, 17th edition, Methuen, 1926, p. 142. Against this quotation may be set one from a piece of fiction written by a scientist. In Fred Hoyle's novel *The Black Cloud* (Penguin Books, 1960, p. 130), a civil servant tells the Prime Minister, 'scientists don't claim to be infallible . . . it's really we laymen who attach infallibility to their statements'.

5. F. R. Jevons, *The Biochemical Approach to Life*, 2nd edition, Allen and Unwin, 1968, chapter 5.

6. R. Gilpin, *American Scientists and Nuclear Weapons Policy*, Princeton University Press, paperback edition, 1965, p. 21.

7. The text of the Franck Report is printed in R. Jungk, *Brighter than a Thousand Suns*, Penguin Books, 1960, p. 311.

8. U.S. Department of State, *A Report on the International Control of Atomic Energy*, U.S.G.P.O., 1946, pp. xi-xii; quoted in Gilpin (note 6 above), pp. 58-9. For further comments, see F. R. Jevons, 'Politicians and Scientists', *Physics Bulletin* 19, 42-5 (1968).

9. M. Polanyi, *Personal Knowledge*, Routledge and Kegan Paul, 1958. A shorter version is, however, available in the book given in note 3 above.

10. A. Koestler, *The Sleepwalkers*, Penguin Books, 1964; *The Act of Creation*, Pan Books, 1966.

11. K. Popper, *Conjectures and Refutations*, 2nd edition, Routledge and Kegan Paul, 1965.

12. Committee on Manpower Resources for Science and Technology, *Report on the 1965 Triennial Manpower Survey of Engineers, Technologists, Scientists and Technical Supporting Staff*, Cmnd. 3103, H.M.S.O., 1966, paragraph 11.

13. P. B. Medawar, *The Art of the Soluble*, Methuen, 1967, p. 87. The general principle 'that one should go for the best combination of probability and value' is discussed by D. E. Broadbent, 'Aspects of Human Decision-Making', *Advancement of Science*, September 1967, p. 53.

14. H. A. Krebs, 'The Making of a Scientist', *Nature* 215, 1441 (1967). The point is part of Krebs's case for encouraging centres of excellence where scientists are kept largely free of burdens of

teaching, administration, etc. He argues that research requires a high minimum critical effort to be effective, just as an aircraft needs a minimum critical speed to become airborne, and that for this reason a worker cannot do half as much research if he cuts down the time he spends on it by half. This is quite true, but the reasons need looking into. The effect of distraction on individual performance could be a part-explanation, but it could also work the other way; inspiration has been known to come when least looked for, and teaching can help to keep a strong and broad grasp of the fundamentals of a subject. There is one factor which is quite simple and quite tangible. Since other workers in the field do not slow down by half, there is still just as much to keep abreast of, and success in science depends on being the first to do something in the face of international competition (cf. note 17 below).

15. D. J. de Solla Price, *Little Science, Big Science*, Columbia University Press, paperback edition, 1965. For reservations regarding the interpretation of figures on exponential growth, however, see S. P. R. Rose, 'The S-curve Considered', *Technology and Society*, vol. 4, no. 1, pp. 33-9, 1968.

16. A. N. Whitehead, *Science and the Modern World*, New American Library, 1948, p. 51.

17. As Medawar (note 13 above, pp. 94 and 86) says: 'A scientist's concern about matters of priority may not be creditable, but only prigs deny its existence, and the fact that it does exist points to something distinctive in the act of creation as it occurs in science ... Artists are not troubled by matters of priority'. On simultaneous discovery, see also R. K. Merton, 'Priorities in Scientific Discovery', in *The Sociology of Science* (edited by B. Barber and W. Hirsch), Free Press of Glencoe, 1962, pp. 447-85.

18. Price (note 15 above), p. 40.

19. Kuhn (note 2 above), p. 20.

20. A. N. Whitehead, *The Aims of Education and Other Essays*, Williams and Norgate, first published in 1932 and many times reprinted.

21. A readable account is given by L. Hudson in *Contrary Imaginations*, Methuen, 1966, chapter 6.

Notes to Pages 44-53

22. Kuhn, in the book cited in note 2 above.

23. A. Koestler, *The Act of Creation*, Pan Books, 1966; cf. section 2b.

24. M. Polanyi, *Minerva* 1, 54 (1962).

25. J. Needham, 'Science and Society in East and West', in *The Science of Science*, edited by M. Goldsmith and A. Mackay, Penguin Books, 1966, p. 162.

26. R. K. Merton, 'Science and Economy of Seventeenth-Century England', in *The Sociology of Science* (note 17 above), pp. 67-88. A modern version of the issue is the discussion by economists of the 'demand-pull' and 'technology-push' views of inventive activity (see F. M. Scherer, 'Firm Size, Market Structure, Opportunity and the Output of Patented Inventions', *American Economic Review* 55, 1097-1125 (1965)). Cf. also note 52 to chapter 3.

27. B. H. Flowers, in *Industry and the Universities—Aspects of Interdependence*, Association of Commonwealth Universities, 1966, p. 23. This is the report of the proceedings of a conference convened by the Committee of Vice-Chancellors and the Confederation of British Industry.

28. The figures are taken from *Statistics of Science and Technology* produced jointly by the Department of Education and Science and the Ministry of Technology, H.M.S.O., S.O. Code No. 27-407, 1967, Table 1, and from the Council for Scientific Policy's *Report on Science Policy*, Cmnd. 3007, H.M.S.O., 1966, Appendix I. Reservations regarding the reliability for comparisons of figures for total research and development expenditure in 1955-6 are made on p. 5 of *Statistics*. A breakdown into categories of research (*Statistics*, Tables 2, 4 and 6) may help to put matters into perspective. In 1964-5, current expenditure (that is, expenditure after deducting capital spending on land, buildings and equipment) was £655 million. Of this, £82 million was devoted to research classified as basic, the biggest contribution to this total being the £37 million spent in universities and technical colleges. Research classified as applied accounted for £171 million and development for £402 million. In these two categories, the lion's share of the work was done in private industry, although much of the finance came from Government departments (see note 49 to chapter 3).

29. *Report on Science Policy* (note 28 above), paragraph 9.

30. Committee on Manpower Resources for Science and Technology, *Interim Report of the Working Group on Manpower Parameters for Scientific Growth*, Cmnd. 3102, H.M.S.O., 1966, paragraph 33. The shortage of able graduates to teach science in schools may be even more serious than deficiencies in industry. Full documentation for the 'starving of industry and schools' is given in the final Swann Report (*The Flow into Employment of Scientists, Engineers and Technologists*, H.M.S.O., Cmnd. 3760, 1968).

31. 'Astryx', in *Times Educational Supplement*, January 12, 1968.

Chapter Three

1. Galileo wrote this to Belisario Vinta, secretary of state in Florence; the letter is quoted in S. Drake, *Discoveries and Opinions of Galileo*, Doubleday Anchor Books, 1957, p. 63.

2. A. Koestler, *The Sleepwalkers*, Penguin Books, 1964.

3. L. Geymonat, *Galileo Galilei*, McGraw-Hill, 1965. See especially p. 58 and p. 71.

4. See F. R. Jevons, 'Brecht's Life of Galileo and the Social Relations of Science', *Technology and Society*, vol. 4, no. 3, pp. 26-9, 1968.

5. Popper (note 11 to chapter 2), chapter 3, 'Three Views Concerning Human Knowledge'.

6. Letter to Foscarini, quoted in Drake (note 1 above), p. 163. There are many accounts of the astronomical issues — for instance, in Koestler (note 2 above) and in T. S. Kuhn, *The Copernican Revolution*, Harvard University Press, 1957.

7. R. K. Merton, 'Science and the Social Order', in *The Sociology of Science* (note 17 to chapter 2), pp. 16-28; see especially p. 18.

8. J. S. Huxley, *Soviet Genetics and World Science*, Chatto and Windus, 1949, especially pp. 37-44. See also section 3g and Ashby (note 45 below).

9. C. Zirkle, *Death of a Science in Russia*, University of Pennsylvania Press, 1949.

Notes to Pages 65-74

10. The letter is printed in Drake (note 1 above), pp. 175-216; see especially pp. 192-3.

11. J. G. Crowther, *Francis Bacon, The First Statesman of Science*, Cresset Press, 1960.

12. B. Farrington, *Francis Bacon, Philosopher of Industrial Science*, Collier Books, 1961, p. 16.

13. *Francis Bacon*, edited by A. Johnston, Batsford, 1965, pp. 13-15.

14. Printed in Johnston (note 13 above), pp. 161-81; see especially p. 174 onwards.

15. Bacon, *Novum Organum*, Book I, aphorism 3. A modern reprint of the *New Organon*, edited by F. H. Anderson, is published by Bobbs-Merrill, 1960.

16. *Novum Organum*, Book I, aphorism 99.

17. *Novum Organum*, Book II, aphorisms 11-20. Actually, he craved an 'indulgence of the understanding' only after knocking down the first fourteen hypotheses.

18. Darwin is an outstanding example. 'I worked on true Baconian principles, and without any theory collected facts on a wholesale scale' (*The Autobiography of Charles Darwin*, edited by N. Barlow, Collins, 1958, p. 119). It may be worth mentioning that this was written some forty years after the event, and that unaided introspection is in any case often unreliable. Some people might argue that to deny the possibility of gathering facts without assumptions is over-subtle, and that the inductive picture of science is near enough to what sometimes happens to serve for most purposes other than philosophical discussion. I have tried to explain in section 2b why it seems to me to be bad to accept this too readily.

19. *Novum Organum*, Book I, aphorism 61.

20. J. D. Bernal, *The Social Function of Science*, Routledge, 1939, p. 9. This work pioneered the field. Perhaps its openly left-wing sympathies prevent it from getting quite as wide a readership as it deserves. It has been reprinted by the M.I.T. Press, 1967, and the collection of essays edited by Goldsmith and Mackay (note 25 to chapter 2) was a tribute to mark its twenty-fifth anniversary.

Notes to Pages 75-77

21. In 1927, the Bishop of Ripon, preaching the British Association sermon, suggested that 'the sum of human happiness outside scientific circles would not necessarily be reduced if for ten years every physical and chemical laboratory were closed' (Bernal, note 20 above, p. 2). After Hiroshima and Nagasaki, there were calls of 'who is going to stop the scientists?' from those who were content to attribute the blame rather than take the trouble to apportion it. But nowadays such calls to suppress science seem to be drowned in a world-wide chorus of demands for more scientists and technologists to deliver the goods.

22. Huxley (note 8 above), p. 46. In another version of the story, in which the questioner was a politician, the answer was, 'some day you'll tax it'.

23. See note 47 below.

24. High energy physics is one of the fields discussed by A. M. Weinberg in 'Criteria for Scientific Choice', *Minerva* 1, 159 (1963). This article has been much admired, and deservedly so.

25. F. R. Jevons, 'How Valuable is Biochemistry?', *New Scientist*, February 3, 1966. Even the *Report of the Working Group on Molecular Biology* of the Council for Scientific Policy (Cmnd. 3675, H.M.S.O., 1968, paragraph 2) claims only that social and economic dividends are 'likely'.

26. The standard of scientific journalism is in some ways higher in the United States of America than in Britain, though it is improving here. Of course, high-powered scientific journalism is not an unmixed blessing. Scientists working in 'glamour' areas often raise a laugh by saying that they read about developments in their field in the *New York Times* long before they reach the professional journals. If this became true on a large scale, it would not be good, because scrutiny by referees and editors of reputable scientific journals acts as a valuable safety barrier. 'The story of the fundamental experiment on "charge independence", that got into the *New York Times* and seemed to promise a Nobel Prize, but was not confirmed by a later experiment with better "statistics", brings a blush to many a cheek!' (Ziman, note 1 to chapter 2, p. 44; see also p. 111). A safer function for scientific journalism is to bring to a wider audience some of what has gone through the normal vetting procedure of the scientific community.

Notes to Pages 77-85

27. A. M. Weinberg, 'Criteria for Scientific Choice II The Two Cultures', *Minerva* 3, 3 (1964).

28. C. Bibby, letter in *The Times Educational Supplement*, September 22, 1967. Shades of T. H. Huxley! Huxley was himself a fine popularizer of science and an eloquent champion of the role of science in education—see, for instance, 'A Liberal Education and where to find it' and 'Scientific Education' in *Lay Sermons, Addresses and Reviews*, Macmillan, 1883, pp. 27-53 and 54-71. See also W. Irvine, *Apes, Angels and Victorians*, McGraw Hill, 1955, chapter 16, 'The Educator'. Dr. Bibby is himself a biographer of Huxley, but one cannot accuse him of being out of touch with modern education—he is Principal of Kingston-upon-Hull College of Education.

29. Conant (note 1 to chapter 2), p. 23.

30. Bacon's essay 'Of Studies', in Johnston (note 13 above), p. 101.

31. I have a theory, unsubstantiated except for a few outstanding examples in my personal acquaintance, that chemists are specially good at remembering people's names and faces. Could this, if true, be connected with the similarity between this skill and that of remembering names of compounds and their formulae? Such connections need not, of course, be causal ones exerted through education. They may be due to the tendency of people with certain kinds of predisposition or innate ability to choose certain subjects.

32. R. M. Beard, *Research into Teaching Methods in Higher Education*, Society for Research into Higher Education, London, 1967, p. 2 and p. 42.

33. W. James, *The Times*, September 30, 1967. Strictly, all that one can deduce is that the selection procedure is equally effective with applicants from all courses in picking people that do well in the Civil Service. More pertinent evidence comes from applicants' success ratios—see section 4g.

34. Hardly any scientists and technologists reach £2,000 a year much before the age of 30, according to the April 1967 Salary Survey of the Graduate Appointments Register, quoted by D. Hutchings, *The Science Undergraduate*, Oxford University Department of Education, 1967, p. 52.

35. I am indebted to an unpublished paper by S. Metcalfe (Research Report No. 8, Department of Liberal Studies in Science, University of Manchester) for a discussion of this point. Briefly, the situation is this. According to classical economic theory, increases in output per head are due to increases in capital per head—that is, economic growth is due to capital accumulation. However, there is an additional factor contributing to increases in output per head, namely 'technical change'. Many calculations indicate that this can outweigh the effects of increase in capital—for instance, by an estimated factor of four in the case of the United States private non-farm sector in the period 1909-49 (R. Solow, 'Technical Change and the Aggregate Production Function', *Review of Economics and Statistics* 39, 312-20 (1957); W. P. Hogan, 'Technical Progress and the Production Function', *Review of Economics and Statistics*, 40, 407-11 (1958)). The 'technical change' component is itself not due entirely to innovation in the sense of the introduction of new products and processes. Economies of scale also contribute, and so do improvements in the quality of labour (due to better education and health) and higher standards of management (by increasing the efficiency with which resources are used) (E. D. Domar, 'On the Measurement of Technological Change', *Economic Journal* 71, 709-29 (1961)). The last two factors indicate some ways in which the elusive 'cultural' benefits of scientific (and other) education overlap with economic ones.

36. The innovations studied are those which in 1966 and 1967 won Queen's Awards to Industry for Technological Innovation. The work is being carried out in the Department of Liberal Studies in Science, University of Manchester, by J. Langrish, M. Gibbons, W. G. Evans and Miss Vivien Seal, and it is supported financially in part by the Council for Scientific Policy.

37. D. J. de Solla Price, 'Is Technology Historically Independent of Science?', *Technology and Culture* 6, 553-67 (1965).

38. B. R. Williams, 'Research and Economic Growth', *Minerva* 3, 57 (1964). For a breakdown of British figures into basic research, applied research and development, see note 28 to chapter 2.

39. See, for instance, the paper by B. R. Williams, cited in the preceding note; also C. F. Carter and B. R. Williams, 'Govern-

ment Scientific Policy and the Growth of the British Economy', *Manchester School* 32, 197-214 (1964), partly reprinted in *Minerva* 3, 114 (1964).

40. This is, of course, apart from the very specialized knowledge specific to the job which can only be picked up on the job, or at least is best picked up there. Such knowledge can be thought of as a high, narrow peak that can often be erected on a rather low-lying plateau of general scientific literacy.

41. J. Langrish (personal communication) has unearthed evidence in the case of one recent commercially successful innovation that the information on which it was based had been buried in a local college for decades. The firm claimed that it had introduced the first new type of product in the field for 150 years. For publicity purposes, it seems to have been considered that new knowledge would carry more prestige than timely and skilful development work which made use of existing knowledge. Surely this is more symptomatic of current attitudes than a reflection of the credit really due to the people concerned for finding the right knowledge at the right time and being able to develop it.

42. I am indebted to another personal communication from J. Langrish for the following example of technology transfer. Disposal of ash from power stations burning pulverized fuel can present a major problem. A possible use for the waste is to sinter it to turn it into a light-weight aggregate for mixing with cement to make concrete. One firm that tried to do this failed, which shows that it was not an easy thing to do. Another firm first made a careful study of the techniques of sintering developed for iron ore, and with this help eventually met with success.

43. See Williams (note 38 above). This paper argues the advantages of importing technological know-how by licences, because such know-how is of proven impact. The limitation here is that licensing agreements sometimes require some know-how in exchange. Skilled manpower is required at home in any case to recognize and absorb the right know-how even if it originates in another firm or country.

44. W. F. Mueller, 'The Origins of the Basic Inventions Underlying Du Pont's Major Product and Process Innovations, 1920 to 1950', in National Bureau of Economic Research, *The Rate and Direction of Inventive Activity*, Princeton University Press,

1962, pp. 323-46. 'Du Pont's management must be commended . . . for continually looking outside as well as within Du Pont's laboratories' (p. 345).

45. E. Ashby, *Scientist in Russia*, Penguin, 1947, p. 101. See also notes 8 and 9 above. The point was brought home to me more recently in a way that is totally devoid of sinister implications but reflects an honest difference of approach. At a talk given in the Department of Chemistry at Manchester, a Russian visitor described a new chromatographic system for separating antibiotics from the many other compounds also present in the culture fluid in which the antibiotic-forming mould has grown. A western worker would probably have first tested the system and tried to get some understanding of the factors involved in its operation by using it on a series of simple model compounds. He might, of course, have spent so long doing this that he would never have got round to trying it on compounds used in industry. The Russian workers, however, appeared only to have used it directly on culture fluids.

46. A. P. Rowe, 'From Scientific Idea to Practical Use', *Minerva* 2, 303 (1964). I have referred in this book mostly to physical science and its application in industry, but similar strains and stresses operate in the life sciences with regard to possible applications in industry or elsewhere, such as in medicine. Many workers in basic life sciences hold aloof from medical applications; they pride themselves on adopting different criteria of merit and sometimes enjoy a good laugh at the medicos on that score, though more so while safe within the faculties of science than when on the operating table.

47. H. S. Lipson, letter to *The Guardian*, July 20, 1968. The point at issue was the British Government's decision (supported by Professor Lipson but bitterly criticized by others) not to participate in the scheme for a European 300 GeV accelerator estimated to cost £150 million.

48. *Statistics* (note 28 to chapter 2), Table 28. The actual figures given are that 23,341 out of 92,494 engineers and technologists, and 18,444 out of 34,599 scientists, are classified as engaged on research and development. The corresponding figures for Government employment are 4,633 out of 20,419 engineers and technologists, and 7,447 out of 11,964 scientists. The qualifications

NOTES TO PAGE 95

considered include not only degrees and Diplomas in Technology but also associateships of certain educational institutions and graduate membership of certain professional bodies. Omissions from the coverage of the survey include agriculture, the armed forces and very small establishments.

The report on *Technological Innovation in Britain* by the Central Advisory Council for Science and Technology (H.M.S.O., 1968) argues that research and development effort in Britain, far from being too low, is proportionately too high, in terms both of expenditure and of utilization of qualified manpower. Thus, in private manufacturing industry, the total investment in new plant and machinery has been only about three times that on research and development. 'This is far too small a ratio, overall, for really effective conversion of R and D projects into commercially fruitful innovations' (paragraph 27). Correspondingly, in manpower terms, it seems that relatively fewer qualified people are engaged in production, management, technical sales and marketing than in some other advanced countries. 'Britain appears to use only about half as many professionally trained people as, for example, Germany in applying science and technology to production and marketing, even though it has many more trying to generate new scientific and technological knowledge' (paragraph 29). See also note 23 to chapter 5.

49. *Statistics* (note 28 to chapter 2) again provides some illuminating facts and figures. During the year 1964-5, the British Government paid £183 million to private industry for research and development (Table 4). Aircraft development accounted for £117 million, much of it, of course, coming through military and defence channels (Tables 9 and 11). The Government itself has been spending £40 to £50 million a year all through the nineteen-sixties on civil atomic energy research and development (Table 15), but this industry's export record is much bleaker than that in aircraft and 'to say that Britain generates more nuclear power electricity than any other single country is a pretty hollow boast if it is also more expensive than anywhere else' (*The Observer*, July 28, 1968). Some benefits will, on the other hand, accrue from these expenditures in indirect and longer-term ways such as technological 'fall-out' or 'spin-off'. There is thus room for a great deal of disagreement about

the economic pros and cons, and the only point I want to insist on here is the general one that research does not generate wealth merely by being 'applied' rather than pure.

50. J. Jewkes, D. Sawers and R. Stillerman (*The Sources of Invention*, Macmillan, revised edition, 1962) seem to have been of the opinion, on the basis of their study of a number of major twentieth century inventions, that the uncertainties surrounding invention are so great that individual inventors can hold their own against organized research by teams in industry. Others, however, emphasize the growing predominance of corporate over private invention (for instance, C. Freeman, 'Science and Economy at the National Level', paper presented at the Experimental Working Session on Science Policy, Paris, February, 1967). J. Schmookler shows that the percentage of U.S. patents awarded to individuals rather than firms declined from 81% at the beginning of the century to 36% in 1956-60 (*Invention and Economic Growth*, Harvard University Press, 1966, p. 26). He points out, however, that patents granted to corporations are often not the result of genuinely corporate research or even of research done within the corporations.

51. C. F. Carter and B. R. Williams, *Industry and Technical Progress*, Oxford University Press, 1957, especially chapter 12, 'Receptive and Efficient Management'. There was a positive correlation between technical progressiveness and the use of scientists and technologists on the Boards of Directors of the firms studied, but it was very imperfect and there were cases suggesting the opposite relation. 'It is simple-minded to suggest that any firm can become progressive merely by drafting a scientist on to the Board'. Such representation is not necessarily a measure of the effectiveness of participation in policy-making by the research staff; participation can be effective without, or ineffective with it.

These conclusions are not really surprising when one thinks about them. It is not difficult to think of ways in which scientist-directors could jeopardize commercial success by pressing too hard for what is 'technically sweet'. Hard-headed businessmen are well aware that it is easy to go broke in the process of pushing through a technological revolution—a reflection at the level of the individual firm of the fact that technological progressiveness

Notes to Page 97

does not always pay. Carter and Williams call this 'receptive but inefficient' management.

52. J. Langrish (Research Report No. 7, Department of Liberal Studies in Science, University of Manchester, 1968, and personal communication). The question at issue is, what was the starting point (in so far as it can be identified) of the research and development work that led to successful commercial use? According to one type of model, a discovery is made first and ultimately finds successful application. According to a second type, popular among industrial managers, a need is first defined, followed by targeted research to meet the need, new discoveries often being made in the process. These two types can be called 'discovery-oriented' and 'need-oriented', or 'push' and 'pull' models respectively (cf. note 26 to chapter 2). Clearly the categorization raises difficulties, but it is not impossible to apply in practice. Out of 14 successful innovations (note 36 above) examined by Langrish in this light, only one resembled the first type and only four the second. In eight of the remainder, the starting point of the innovation was that it was seen that both need and technical possibility existed; development work was accordingly initiated and led to commercial success.

53. L. Bagrit, *The Age of Automation* (The Reith Lectures for 1964), Penguin Books, 1966, pp. 44-5.

54. D. K. Price, *Government and Science*, New York University Press, 1954, p. 187. I have tried to bring out the intricacy of intermingling between technical and political considerations in a discussion (Jevons, note 8 to chapter 2) of points made by Gilpin (note 6 to chapter 2, especially pp. 15-23 and p. 167). Data on the number of deaths to be expected due to radioactive fall-out from nuclear tests were presented in different ways by Pauling and Teller. Pauling, of course, was very much in favour of a ban on tests, Teller was against. Pauling gave the absolute number of deaths to be expected; Teller presented the same data as the number of days lost per life for the American people as a whole due to fall-out relative to the shortening of life due to smoking.

The point here may seem a very elementary one—just a matter of how the presentation of the facts is slanted. One can get examples of that on any day by comparing the presentation of

Notes to Page 97

news items in newspapers of different political persuasions. There is no need actually to distort the facts; one only has to select and emphasize them differently.

But the real issue is rather more subtle. It concerns the possibility of presenting the facts genuinely unslanted. Scientists—and politicians too—have acted (according to Gilpin, at least) as though technical information can be given in a purely objective way, free of any non-technical assumptions or biases, so as to leave it entirely to the decision-makers to combine the technical data with non-technical ingredients in policy formulation. The simple example of the data on the effects of fall-out shows that in practice it is difficult, if not impossible, to draw such a clear dividing line between the technical and political realms. Anybody who feels that only one of the ways of presenting the data is biased should ask himself if he is not just betraying his own bias in the opposite direction.

Perhaps the nearest approach to presenting the evidence in a purely objective way would be to give the expected mortality due to fall-out together with expected mortalities due to other factors, including bigger and smaller factors in equal numbers. Even then, however, some subjectivity is bound to intrude in the selection of the factors.

In a more obviously practical context, Gilpin argues that it can be harmful to assume that science and politics are separable by analyzing the 1958 Geneva Conference on a nuclear test ban. 'The consequences of the belief that the technical and political realms could be isolated from one another are most evident in the American participation in the Geneva Conference of Experts. This failing ... was to be costly for national policy and the unity of the scientific community' (p. 200).

Some people feel that, while it may be difficult to free scientific advice from political bias, the converse is all too easy. Political decisions are made without taking the relevant scientific considerations adequately into account. Scientists who have advised Governments have been known to complain in a disillusioned way afterwards that they were never asked for advice until only one course of action was left open. In other words, the experts were used to justify or 'legitimize' decisions and make them seem respectable after they had already been taken on other grounds.

NOTES TO PAGES 98-100

55. Conant (note 1 to chapter 2), pp. 17-19. Conant was president of Harvard University and war-time Chairman of the U.S. National Defence Research Committee, which was concerned, above all else, with the atom bomb; cf. section 5k.

56. C. P. Snow, *The Two Cultures, and a Second Look*, Cambridge University Press, 1965. Part I is the Rede Lecture, 1959.

57. It seems that the impressive rise of the German chemical industry in the nineteenth century can be traced at least in part to such an apparent surplus of chemists. More chemists were trained than could find employment strictly as chemists, so some of the surplus went into business in the chemical industry and in many cases started new firms themselves, adopting the role of entrepreneurs.

The Swann Report (note 30 to chapter 2, paragraph 99) notes the 'tendency to more general employment of scientists and technologists . . . it is vital, in our view, that it should grow; and we are strengthened in this opinion by the evidence of U.S. practice. Research and development do not of themselves generate wealth, and it is in the later stages of the productive process that by far the greatest expenditure is incurred. It is essential that scientists and technologists, and particularly the most able graduates, should be used more widely in these later stages, and in managerial and administrative roles.'

Chapter Four

1. Elsewhere (F. R. Jevons, 'Science Greats', *The Listener*, May 11, 1967), I have used the Copernican Revolution to illustrate the apparent paradox—quite easy to see through—that the most specialized activities may unavoidably have the most generalized effects. Mathematical astronomy has been advanced since antiquity; it had reached a high degree of intellectual sophistication by the time of Ptolemy in the second century A.D. In the sixteenth century, Copernicus wrote in this connection that 'mathematics are for mathematicians' (*De Revolutionibus Orbium Coelestium*, prefatory letter, in Kuhn, note 6 to chapter 3, p. 142). This is surely an outstanding example of a momentous half-truth. The book which contained it was in fact very much one of technical astronomy, meant for specialist astronomers. Yet it turned out quite soon that Copernican astronomy was not

to be of interest to astronomers only. Within a century it had sparked off an intellectual revolution which transformed the most fundamental conceptions of the nature of the universe and man's place in it (section 3b).

2. The Dainton Report (Council for Scientific Policy, *Enquiry into the Flow of Candidates in Science and Technology into Higher Education*, H.M.S.O., Cmnd. 3541, 1968), paragraphs 138-9. In about one-tenth of the schools studied, it was two or three years earlier still.

3. Colleges of education and further education establishments are not to be neglected in terms of numbers (Dainton Report, paragraphs 33-8), but they do not exercise the influence that universities do on the shape of sixth form education.

4. Perhaps the most serious fact among all the statistics is one that was uncovered by the Robbins Committee in 1963 and apparently still applies (Dainton Report, paragraphs 137-8)—namely, that some 40% of arts undergraduates took no science subject (other than mathematics) even at 'O' level.

5. Mathematical subjects come in the science category. The proportion of pupils taking mixed science and non-science subjects has been increasing markedly, from 10% for first year sixth formers in 1962 to 16% in 1967 (Dainton Report, Table 1), but such mixtures are still thought of in many schools (though no longer in all) as primarily for weaker pupils not intending to go on to university. In recent years, it has become the practice to distinguish some of the subjects formerly counted as 'arts' in a new group of 'social sciences' (see Dainton Report, annex B); these include not only economics and British constitution but also geography and English economic history. For most purposes in this book, particularly in referring to schools rather than universities, I continue to use the word 'arts' to include such subjects.

6. The Scottish system differs markedly from that in England and Wales in that it provides an unspecialized education up to the Higher grade examinations at the age of about 17. The Dainton Report notes this with approval and hopes that the traditional breadth will be maintained (paragraphs 88-115).

7. See J. K. Brierley, *Science in its Context*, Heinemann, 1964.

Notes to Page 102

One examining board sets an 'A' level paper in General Studies but with nothing that could properly be called a 'syllabus'.

8. A. D. C. Peterson, *Arts and Science Sides in the Sixth Form*, Oxford University Department of Education, 1960; quoted and commented on by J. K. Brierley in The Schools Council, Working Paper No. 4, *Science in the Sixth Form*, H.M.S.O., 1966, S.O. Code No. 27-390-4.

9. Alexander Pope is not as widely recognized as he might be as the poet-philosopher of the English educational system. *The Essay on Criticism* (1711) contains these lines:

> "A little learning is a dang'rous thing;
> Drink deep, or taste not the Pierian spring:
> There shallow draughts intoxicate the brain,
> And drinking largely sobers us again."

10. The Crowther Report (Central Advisory Council for Education (England), 15 to 18, H.M.S.O., 1959) paragraph 385. This report makes better reading and more stimulating intellectual fare than most of the publications of Her Majesty's Stationery Office. Looking back on it after a decade, some people might be tempted to dismiss the chapter on the sixth form curriculum (chapter 25) as a piece of special pleading—but then, most pleading is special and this is at least a particularly accomplished example of the *genre*.

One line of argument proceeds (in what is admittedly a rather self-satisfied way) by pointing out how much worse things are abroad. The width of American high school education, it seems, means that nothing is studied seriously enough. The system in some countries on the continent of Western Europe, on the other hand, makes such heavy demands over so wide a range that it risks overstrain. If a broad curriculum is 'either too superficial or too exhausting, then the field is left clear for the English recipe of specialization'. This is recognized by the authors themselves as 'a palpable debating point'.

The question of 'subject-mindedness' is dealt with in section 4c of this book. Apart from that, there remain three major arguments in the Crowther Report.

Firstly, it is said that a pupil studying a limited field acquires self-confidence in his growing mastery of the subject. This is a good point. But it is dangerous to cultivate the feeling that

Notes to Page 103

mastery of one subject is some sort of excuse for not tackling others which may be important. Self-confidence achieved by choosing to ignore ignorance is too dearly bought.

Secondly, it is said that education should introduce a pupil 'into one or two areas which throw light on the achievement of man'. No educator would quarrel with this (though he might wonder how drastic the difference is between 'one or two' and 'two or three'). Curiously, though, specialization is exemplified by 'the honours school of *Literae Humaniores* (Greats) at Oxford ... With the aid of a precise linguistic discipline, it develops a knowledge of the literature, the history, the art, and the thought of one of the great cultures of the world'. This is just the kind of multidisciplinary approach which present practice rarely encourages and often prevents, especially on the science side (see section 4e).

Thirdly, it is said that mental growth and ripening depend on a close personal relation of 'intellectual discipleship' between pupils and teacher, which takes 'many hours together' to develop. It is not clear exactly how many hours per week over two years are required, at a minimum; nor is it clear that there might not be advantages in variety if no single teacher is so outstanding as to deserve exclusive discipleship.

Having settled firmly for specialization, the Crowther Report enlarges on giving literacy to science specialists and numeracy to arts specialists. Here it is most perceptive about the ends, though partly unrealistic about the means (use of minority time). By literacy the authors mean not only ability to use the mother tongue but also development of moral, aesthetic and social judgment. By numeracy (the word is of their own coinage) they mean not only ability to reason quantitatively but also some acquaintance with the methods and achievements of science.

11. 'Towards a Broader Curriculum', *Nature* 215, 1329 (1967).
12. The Schools Council, Working Papers No. 5, *Sixth Form Curriculum and Examinations*, 1966, and No. 16, *Some Further Proposals for Sixth Form Work*, 1967, H.M.S.O., S.O. Code Nos. 27-390-5 and 88-5370-16 respectively.
13. Dainton Report (note 2 above), opposite p. 1.
14. D. Hutchings, *Technology and the Sixth Form Boy*, Oxford University Department of Education, 1963.

15. There is an interesting comparison here with some subjects outside the natural sciences. University appointments officers find that graduates in psychology or sociology, for instance, are in a way at a disadvantage in getting their first jobs because they tend to feel that they have some useful skill that they ought to be able to sell on the employment market, whereas a graduate in history or classics is well aware that (unless he is going to teach his subject) he has nothing to offer other than his 'well-trained mind'. The 'vocational' element bears little relation to educational specialization. As far as course contents go, history or classics may well be more specialized than psychology or sociology. See also note 32 below.

16. Crowther Report (note 10 above), paragraph 387.

17. J. R. Butler, *Occupational Choice*, Department of Education and Science, Science Policy Studies No. 2, H.M.S.O., 1968, S.O. Code No. 27-418-2.

18. Dainton Report (note 2 above), paragraphs 126-44.

19. L. Hudson, *Contrary Imaginations*, Methuen, 1966.

20. Hudson, p. 41.

21. Hudson, p. 157. Among girls, it seems that the correlation between convergence-divergence and science-arts specialization is if anything weaker, though complications arise in making the comparison (L. Hudson, *Frames of Mind*, Methuen, 1968, p. 23).

22. Price (note 15 to chapter 2), p. 11.

23. Price (note 15 to chapter 2, p. 53) suggests that 'the total number of scientists goes up as the square, more or less, of the number of good ones'.

24. Medawar (note 13 to chapter 2), p. 114.

25. The argument that is sometimes used—more frequently, it seems, by chemists than by physicists or biologists—is that there is a certain amount of stuff that ought to be 'got through' for a degree. For reservations about this, see section 4f. Even if the argument is accepted strictly at face value, it is instructive to do an order-of-magnitude calculation on it. Chemistry at 'A' level is typically taken as one of three subjects for two years; that makes it equivalent to two terms full-time. An undergraduate chemist usually spends well over half his course time on chemistry itself; say that this is equivalent to five terms full-time. Even

if school chemistry were slashed by half, the total exposure time between 'O' level and first degree would be cut by only one-seventh. Since the rate of learning is not likely to be uniform—at least it *should* be or *could* be greater at university—the total amount of chemistry learned might be affected even less. (It should be quite clear that the line of argument about the amount of material to be covered is *not* the same as that which insists that physics or chemistry cannot be started properly without an adequate grounding in mathematics. This difficulty is a real one, though even it would not be quite as serious as it is if conventions about what constitutes university-level work could be more freely swept away.)

26. See F. R. Jevons, 'The Content of Science Courses', *Higher Education Review*, January, 1969.

27. Chemistry is a good example. It has a reassuringly single-barrelled name, but doubts have nevertheless been expressed even in high places about the degree to which there is genuine intellectual coherence between its organic and physical branches.

There might be one possible way to get some kind of operational measure of subject boundaries. One might try to assess over what areas research workers show mutual dependence on each other. This could be measured, albeit imperfectly, by the extent to which they cite work by each other in their publications. (The *Science Citation Index* would be a useful tool here; it lists all cited papers, however old, and against each all the current papers which cite it.) Since workers are likely to cite each other the more frequently, the more closely related the areas in which they are working, one could, in principle at least, identify degrees of relationship between sectors.

It might turn out that one can identify only research fronts in certain tightly knit subject fields (D. J. de Solla Price, 'Networks of Scientific Papers', *Science* 149, 510-15 (1965); J. Margolis, 'Citation Indexing and Evaluation of Scientific Papers', *Science* 155, 1213-1219 (1967)). These would reflect groupings of workers at the research front within which 'interbreeding' of ideas, techniques and facts regularly takes place. Teaching subjects, however, are much wider and might therefore still remain arbitrary in extent.

There is an analogy here to biological classification. Only one level of classification has an operational basis — the species. Although there are difficulties in practice, it can be defined in terms of actual or potential interbreeding or a common gene pool. Other levels of classification — varieties, genera, families, orders, classes, phyla—are based on arbitrary criteria.

28. See Jevons (note 5 to chapter 2).

29. See note 10 above.

30. See the Foreword to this book. The type of depth that comes from looking at something in more than one way might perhaps be called 'stereoscopic depth'. This analogy has the advantage of an extra dimension over 'redrawing the map of learning'.

31. See note 4 above.

32. There is a great deal of woolly thinking about the relation between 'specialist' and 'vocational' education. The following is an example. Commenting on the impending demise of the amateur from the administrative class of the Civil Service (as heralded in the Fulton Report), *The Times Educational Supplement* ('Comment', June 28, 1968) professed to be puzzled by the implications for education. 'A minority of the committee cogently remarked that the demand for specialization implicit in the majority's report ran contrary to current opinion at the Schools Council and in the Dainton report. "Despecialization" is the key-word now, yet the Fulton committee seems to favour more, and better, specialization for the administrative grade.' The writer concludes as follows. 'If the balance, both at school and university, is nicely set between the purely academic and the purely vocational or specialized, the Civil Service will get the kind of "professional" administrators it now wants.'

There is a confused antithesis here. The writer implies an inverse correlation between vocational specialization and academic mind-building which does not exist in any strict sense. Not all specialization is vocational—the pressures to specialize arise more inside than outside the academic sphere; nor do all vocational studies lack mind-training qualities.

The real question about specialized education for administration is not so much how far it would be desirable as how far it is actually possible to do anything effective about it. The value of academic knowledge as a guide to action is subject to severe limitations. There is a tendency, inevitable and justified in its

Notes to Pages 121-123

own way, for universities to make subjects into academic disciplines rather than collections of rules of thumb. Even when education tries to be vocational, it cannot achieve more than a very imperfect coverage of what the corresponding jobs require. This applies even in areas like the physical and life sciences where, by general assent, knowledge is most advanced and should therefore have the greatest power to give command over events. Any good engineer will say that there is more to engineering than applied physics, and some would go so far as to say that the real interest and challenge start only where the applied physics stops. As regards the life sciences, it is debatable whether medicine is more a science than an art, and it is quite clear that agriculture remains basically the craft that it always was, however much improved by science. The extent to which the behavioural, social and environmental sciences are of help in actually handling people and societies is all the more open to question. See also note 15 above, and section 5b.

33. See note 10 above, and also section 4e.

34. C. H. Dodd, 'Recruitment to the Administrative Class, 1960-64', *Public Administration*, Spring 1967, p. 55.

35. The issue of specialists *versus* generalists in administration has a significance beyond science and technology; it concerns other kinds of specialists as well—architects, accountants, surveyors and so forth (see F. F. Ridley (editor), *Specialists and Generalists*, Allen and Unwin, 1968). It helps, in the first place, to distinguish clearly between specialization in education and specialization in employment (see note 23 to chapter 5). There then emerge two related questions: to what extent is specialization in education a good way to train minds, and to what extent do specialized jobs early in a career form a good route to top jobs later? Top jobs themselves are not specialist almost by definition, because they cover wide areas of responsibility. The Permanent Secretary of a Ministry has to cope with more than one type of issue, just like his counterparts in politics and business, the Cabinet Minister and the chairman of a large company. Indeed, one of the principal requirements for such positions is skill in reconciling different kinds of considerations.

Legal training is a common route to high administrative positions in some countries on the continent of Europe, but it seems that law courses adopt a correspondingly broad approach; not designed specifically for sitting in lawyers' offices, they may include substantial infusions of philosophy, politics or economics. Similarly with the widely admired French technocrats, whose education goes far beyond engineering in a strictly professional sense.

36. Dainton Report (note 2 above), paragraphs 44 and 120, figures 3 and 5.

37. Butler (note 17 above), paragraph 74.

38. See note 5 above. One might be tempted to suggest that, the Crowther Report having proclaimed the 'subject-mindedness' of sixth formers, the young are once again concerned to prove officialdom wrong.

39. Dainton Report, paragraphs 121 and 122.

40. W. A. Pullman ('A levels and Engineering as a Career', *The Chartered Mechanical Engineer*, June 1968, p. 260) suggests as one possibility 'the establishment of new universities in rural areas away from industry and technology'.

41. See notes 15 and 32 above.

42. J. Wren-Lewis, *The Guardian*, February 23, 1965.

43. Dainton Report, paragraph 119.

44. Dainton Report, paragraph 157. See also section 5e.

45. Dainton Report, summary of recommendations, opposite p. 1.

46. There have been and are university 'conversion courses' to turn arts sixth formers into science or technology graduates, but none so far has made a major impact.

47. Commenting on a useful short summary of recent reports (Council of Engineering Institutions, *Engineers, Technologists and Scientists in the National Economy*, 1968), *The Times Educational Supplement* ('Astryx', June 14, 1968) pointed out how much it has become conventional wisdom to bemoan Britain's shortage of scientists and technologists. 'This is a dogma which it is almost heresy to doubt. Yet the real evidence for it is very difficult to find. If there were a shortage in the economic sense, the salaries of such men would have rocketed.' One is told that a young man with the humblest kind of degree in almost any kind of engineering can get half a dozen offers of jobs with-

out difficulty. Perhaps the paradox might clear up if one were to look at the *kinds* of jobs he is offered, and their prospects.

48. Once again I point to the statistic of note 4 above.

49. The Dainton Report recognizes this (paragraph 167). One way of illustrating the need for scientific background in 'all-rounders' is as follows. The questions on which the diverger (the alleged arts type—see section 4c) does well are 'open-ended' ones of the kind, 'how many uses can you think of for a brick?' We could do with more people who are good at thinking of uses for scientific and technological bricks such as lasers or transistors.

50. A. H. Jennings, reported in *Nature*, note 11 above.

51. The Dainton Report commented on the advantages of the compactness which the existence of only one examining board gives the Scottish system and which made possible a 'quite remarkable' speed and comprehensiveness in changing to new syllabuses (paragraph 107). The methods by which France, alone in Western Europe, has managed to expand the share of science and technology in education, 'in particular the institutional controls . . . obviously merit further study' (paragraph 125).

52. Possibly the case of mathematics is special—not just as special as every other case but so *very* special that it really does deserve special treatment. High-level mathematical ability is a rather unique kind of gift which can be identified at an early age, and mathematicians' real originality flowers early. So there is perhaps a case for special schools where those with exceptional mathematical gifts can be allowed to forge ahead fast, without necessarily devoting an exorbitantly large proportion of their time to mathematics. Perhaps, instead of filling our boarding schools with a 50 per cent quota of pupils selected for a relatively nebulous 'boarding need' (as the Public Schools Commission recommended in 1968), we could make just a very small number of them into special schools for the real high flyers in mathematics; in other words, we could recognize outstanding mathematical gifts as one type of 'boarding need'. If so, it should be for a very small and select minority; M. J. Lighthill, who made just this kind of suggestion in a talk broadcast on the B.B.C. Third Programme on September 19, 1966, thought one such school might be enough for Britain.

Chapter Five

1. Of course, specialization is usually done in the name of high standards, and it is true that it is necessary to specialize to attain standards that are high as measured in one way, though that way is not the only possible way. When thinking of standards in subjects, it is salutary to be reminded how little any course covers in any case. At what is probably a generous estimate, two per cent of what is worth knowing in an advanced branch of science such as physics or chemistry can be covered in an intensive honours course. To cut that to one per cent could be thought of as making little difference since it increases the omissions by only one per cent.

2. See note 32 to chapter 4; also chapter 1.

3. *The Times Educational Supplement* is one regular source of comment. I am grateful for a summary of views from industry sent to me by Mr. P. M. Knowlson, secretary of a working party on universities and industrial research set up by the Confederation of British Industry and the Vice-Chancellors under the chairmanship of Mr. P. Docksey.

4. It is argued against examinations that they cause anxiety states because of the artificial stress they create. In this connection, it is pertinent to ask in the first place what it is that is artificial about stress. It is not artificial in the sense that it does not exist in the educational system apart from examinations, or in human societies outside the educational system, or in nature outside human societies (ask the antelope pursued by a lion). The ability to perform well under stress is one of the factors that distinguishes achievement from ability, and sooner or later it must become achievement that counts. There are plenty of people who have brilliant futures behind them because, when it came to the crunch, they could not face stress.

Alternatively, is the stress artificial in the sense that it is different in kind from stresses not connected with examinations? That is not really the case. The ability to master the facts of a situation, given reasonably long notice, and then present them at reasonable speed is one that is demanded in many walks of life. In some ways, indeed, assessment by examinations is more suitable by the standards of life outside the educational system than by internal academic ones (though even academics are not, of course, totally insulated from stress). Surely the whole argument should be directed not against examinations altogether but against exclusive reliance on them for assessment.

5. The Bosworth Report (Committee on Manpower Resources for Science and Technology, *Education and training requirements for the electrical and mechanical manufacturing industries*, H.M.S.O., 1966, S.O. Code No. 27 - 399) discusses the planning of 'matching sections' to bridge the gap between educational supply and industrial needs, particularly for the design and manufacturing functions.

6. See note 42 to chapter 3.

7. See note 32 to chapter 4, and section 4g. There is an intriguing difference in the usage of words between industry and the Civil Service. In industry, the manager takes the high-level decisions and the administrator looks after the details; in the Civil Service, it is the other way round.

8. I owe the expression 'scientific stenography' to an anonymous scribbler on a time-table pinned on a notice-board.

9. It is this follow-up—when it is done—that makes the difference between course reading and 'outside' reading. Hutchings (note 34 to chapter 3, p. 44) believes that science students are not much different from arts students in their outside reading habits during term. It is often painfully obvious, however, that their course reading tends to be largely confined to concentrated study of a small number of highly fact-intensive text-books.

10. This is not to be interpreted as a levelling down of standards. A proper principle in all teaching is to pitch the standard somewhere near the class average, not in the top five per cent of the range. It is easier for supplementary reading to open additional avenues for the high flyers than to plug gaps for students of nearer average ability.

11. The Dainton Report (note 2 to chapter 4) called, in its third main recommendation (opposite p. 1), for 'breadth, humanity and up-to-dateness' to be infused into the science curriculum and its teaching. The question of up-to-dateness is discussed in section 5h.

12. A. Koestler, *The Sleepwalkers*, Penguin Books, 1964 (cf.

Notes to Page 142

sections 2b and 3b); J. D. Watson, *The Double Helix*, Weidenfeld and Nicolson, 1968.

13. To be more specific about the suggested teaching style, I give below a slightly edited version of a document written for use in connection with the 'Science Greats' course run by the Department of Liberal Studies in Science in collaboration with other Departments in the University of Manchester. (For the aims of this course, see the Foreword.) The case is somewhat overstated here, in the hope (not necessarily justified) that this is the way most likely to overcome educational inertia. Like most pronouncements on teaching methods, this one should be considered as no more than a set of suggestions which any individual teacher can consider for incorporation in his own personal teaching style.

PHYSICAL SCIENCE TEACHING FOR SCIENCE GREATS

I suggest that our purposes would be best served if, instead of devoting a lot of effort to defining a range of *teaching matter*, we concentrate in the first instance on finding the best *teaching style*.

We are not unduly worried about the amount of material covered, but very concerned about the skills being developed in the minds of our students. This applies to some extent to all good teaching, of course, but more so to us; so we are readier to sacrifice coverage for the sake of a type of course organization which throws more responsibility on the students to process information themselves. The kind of processing in which we are most interested uses printed material as the predominant form of input. The output takes two main forms:

(i) solving of problems, usually numerical,
(ii) verbal (or predominantly verbal) exposition and discussion of material with a technical content.

I propose that the lecturer asked to give a course should start by forgetting entirely about writing 40 or so lectures in the usual sense. Instead, he should specify in detail a selection of reading material.

Some objections may immediately spring to mind—'teaching from the book', 'abnegating responsibility for teaching', 'a teach-yourself system', etc. I know that university teachers often take pride in the originality of their lectures in terms of the matter they contain and its mode of treatment ('you won't find *my* lectures in any book'). But there is no need for the lecturer to swallow any pride. The teaching problems in the system I envisage are more challenging, not less, than in the traditional system. I just want the lecturer to spare some

Notes to Page 142

of his effort, imagination and ingenuity for things other than the straight presentation of material.

The procedure

1 *Define the reading material*

(i) A 'core' of material that all students are really expected to read thoroughly should be clearly indicated on the reading list and separated from supplementary reading.

(ii) For the system to work, the core material must be *easily* accessible to students. ('Use of library' exercises are not in general suitable for undergraduate classes.) It would be best, therefore, if it could be taken largely from one book, preferably a cheap edition. I know individual books tend to be patchy—but how often is the excellence of individual lecturers more uniform?

(iii) It probably helps (in the sense that it increases the amount of reading that students actually do) to indicate core material quite specifically in terms of chapters or even parts of chapters. This is not spoon-feeding because supplementary reading is open-ended. *Guided reading* is the aim.

(iv) The amount of core material should be severely limited; it should cover *less* than would normally be covered in a course of straight lectures of equivalent length. The lecturer has to exercise strict self-restraint here; the ambition to 'get more in' is misplaced and defeats the main purpose of the exercise.

(v) The supplementary material should *not* consist mainly of more advanced theory, specialist monographs, etc. Discussions of significance and implications of the basic theory, and, in particular, indications of its practical relevance, are probably more profitable. Short articles from the semi-popular or 'applied' literature could find a place here. Such items should not make up the bulk of the reading, but a moderate number of judiciously selected ones scattered through the course (*not* saved up for the end) helps to maintain interest by giving variety to the reading matter and indicating relevance to concrete situations. A few items of this kind could serve as the basis for written exercises, in which case they should really be regarded as additional core items.

2 *Set a series of problems to be solved and questions to be answered*

(i) There might be, say, 100 numerical problems to be solved. (It might be many more, or many fewer.) The number of questions to be answered verbally depends on the length of answer expected—anything from single explanatory sentence to full-blown essay.

(ii) Indications of relevant reading for particular problems and

Notes to Page 142

questions might be appropriate. This is not necessarily spoon-feeding; we want students to get to grips with the material, not stumble around looking for it. Some interesting written work might arise out of the material of 1 (v) above.

(iii) Some weight should be given to verbal answers in the final assessment for the course. Unfortunately, it does not seem feasible to do the same for numerical problems with unique answers.

(iv) In the first year Physics course, Gordon Murray has had success with essays on subjects like:

> equations of state for gases
> liquid helium
> the concept of temperature
> the measurement of e/m.

3 Lectures and classes

(i) The 'course material' is now defined by 1 and 2 above, so the lecturer need not define it by covering it in lectures. He is free to use his scheduled teaching time to help students to acquire it themselves from their own reading. Obviously, he should *not* just take it that students have learned or will learn the stuff from the book so that he is free to talk about something additional or something else instead.

(ii) Some of the teaching could take the form of lectures. I think that most lecturers will want, however, to organize some audience participation and feedback. They would be free within wide limits to decide on the best form that this might take to suit them and their material.

(iii) Some of the lecturing might be pre-reading, to act as *apéritif* for the reading list. Specific comments on sections of it stimulate students to get down to it. With a relatively difficult bit of theory, it might be appropriate to give a very simple discussion introductory to the more formal presentation in a text-book.

(iv) Some lecturing and discussion should, however, be post-reading, on the understanding (and with due warning) that 'you won't get much out of this unless you've read through chapter so-and-so at least once beforehand'. This, together with written work that requires reading beyond the lectures, is the best way of really getting students to read seriously.

(v) The teaching style is, therefore, *reading-based* rather than lecture-based. To encourage reading should be a specific aim, not just a hoped-for side-effect. Experience shows that most students are prepared to do a fair amount of reading, given manageable material and some reasonably specific target such as a piece of written work. It is when they have to scribble down lecture notes and just learn them afterwards that they get fed up, and with some justification. They should not have to depend on lectures as the source of material; the role of the lecturer should be to select reading material for them, to be their helper, interpreter and guide in tackling it and to impose intellectual discipline by checking the accuracy with which they use it.

(vi) Lecturing might highlight topics of particular importance, interest or difficulty. This could be done either pre-reading or post-reading. ('You really must grasp this bit. Will you please get your minds to work on it? I'll go through it with you now/next time.')

(vii) Discussion and written work should serve three main functions:
> to stimulate reading
> to check the effectiveness of reading
> to develop powers of expressing material
> with a technical content.

(viii) Some topics for discussion and written work might be very general. (What is this bit of subject-matter really about? What type of question are we trying to answer and what sort of answer can we give? What can thermodynamics tell us, and what can't it tell us, about chemical reactions?) Others might be very specific (e.g. illustrative cases, worked examples). Some might probe depth of understanding (e.g. 'heat capacity and entropy units both have the dimensions, calories per degree, so what is the difference between them?'). Some might attempt integration with other courses where this is feasible; to do this effectively is a real challenge to the lecturer!

Is it practicable?

(i) The system need not be wildly extravagant on staff time. I am not suggesting a specially tailored course of lectures *plus* tutorials with small groups, but rather a diversion of effort from straight presentation in lectures to other forms of teaching, at least some of which can be done with quite large groups.

(ii) To allay one possible cause of anxiety in the lecturer, let me repeat that he is not forbidden to lecture, only relieved of the necessity to cover all the course material in lecture form.

(iii) Flexibility to meet the spread of student ability is greater for a reading list than for a course of lectures, which is necessarily the same for the whole class. The best students can be given ample scope with the open-ended reading list. The weakest students should be at least as well off as with the traditional system; the core reading list is surely as good a safety net as unreliable and often incomplete notes from imperfectly understood lectures.

Notes to Page 142

(iv) Will students not bother to come to classes? I don't think the difficulty will arise if the lecturer sees his role as 'helper, interpreter and guide'; most students will then be glad to make use of what he provides. If, however, some of them think that they can tackle the reading by themselves, I see no reason why they should be forced to attend. The problems and questions should be compulsory, not attendance.

(v) Whatever one teaches, it is most unlikely to cover the needs of the graduates' future careers. A teaching style which fosters reliance on the printed rather than the spoken word should build up students' ability, willingness and confidence to tackle new subjects and problems.

In practice, people can often appreciate the attractions of the teaching style described above for verbal subject-matter, but find it difficult to see how it can be applied where a great deal depends on mathematical proofs and derivations. No less a person than J. J. Thomson supplies an answer to these doubts in the following passage about his studies at Cambridge (*Recollections and Reflections*, Bell, 1936, pp. 35-9; I am grateful to Mr. A. Armstrong for drawing my attention to this).

'Besides attending lectures on Greek I also, like the great majority of those aspiring to obtain a good place in the Mathematical Tripos, "coached" with Routh, the most famous of mathematical teachers. Routh's teaching was not in the least like what is ordinarily understood by "coaching"; it was in reality a series of exceedingly clear and admirably arranged lectures . . . I had heard so much of Routh's teaching that I went to his class with great expectations. I confess at first I was somewhat disappointed: his lecture was quite clear, but there was nothing particularly novel or striking about what he said, and taking any particular lecture, I had heard as good a one from other teachers. After a short time, however, I began to appreciate their merits . . . In his lectures he took us through the best textbook on the subject, the parts which the author had treated satisfactorily he just told us to read: when the book was obscure he made it plain; when the proof of a theorem was longer than need be he gave us the shortest one; when the author had put in something that was not important he told us not to read it; when he had omitted something that was important he supplied the omissions. These diversions made the lectures more interesting and more easily remembered. His lectures on Rigid Dynamics, on which he had written the standard textbook . . . were not so interesting as those on other subjects. He naturally had not so many opportunities for criticism . . .

Notes to Pages 142-149

'Routh's system certainly succeeded in the object for which it was designed, that of training men to take high places in the tripos; for in the 33 years from 1855 to 1888 in which it was in force, he had 27 Senior Wranglers and he taught 24 in 24 successive years. Results like these could not have been obtained unless he had been a born teacher, as he was, and had spent, as he had, time and labour in keeping his technique up to the mark. . . . Routh . . . was Senior Wrangler in the year when Clerk Maxwell was second.'

14. J. McLeish (*The Lecture Method*, Cambridge Institute of Education, 1968, p. 45) cites a few studies which provide some support for the superiority in certain ways of independent study over the lecture method.

15. Dainton Report, paragraphs 64-66 and 85.

16. Nuffield Foundation, *Chemistry, Handbook for Teachers*, Longmans/Penguin Books, 1967, p. 1. The idea of reform in school science has become identified in the minds of many with the name of the Nuffield Foundation. The Nuffield Science Teaching Project has been a major force in generating enthusiasm, working out ideas and publishing material in this field. A measure of its success is the way that many teachers want to go where Nuffield courses are taught.

17. Even among practising scientists, the degree of patience varies. As is well known, university physicists are not quite as keen on practical work as chemists and biologists are. This may reflect differences in the status accorded to theoreticians in the different fields. In physics, the theoretician is highly regarded, but he occupies a less exalted place among chemists, and in biology he is only just in the process of becoming anything more than a sarcastic joke.

18. Hutchings (note 34 to chapter 3), pp. 37-40. The proportion of students spending more than 20 hours per week in laboratories was highest in the sample from Oxford and Cambridge, where all of them were final year chemists. It was lowest in the sample from Bradford, a newly developing technological university.

19. I am aware that any suggestions for putting the brakes on practical work are not likely to be well received. The idea that there can be improvement without a massive increase in cost is not in tune with the times.

Notes to Pages 150-154

20. A Nuffield 'A' level physical science course started in a few pilot schools in 1966, and at least one examining board is also preparing a syllabus. See 'Physical Science as a Sixth Form Subject', *Association for Science Education Bulletin*, September 1965, pp. 16-32; and J. Spice, 'The Nuffield Physical Science Course', *Conference*, July 1967.

21. 'The gods had condemned Sisyphus to ceaselessly rolling a rock to the top of a mountain, whence the stone would fall back of its own weight. They had thought with some reason that there is no more dreadful punishment than futile and hopeless labour.' A. Camus, *The Myth of Sisyphus*, translated by J. O'Brien, Hamish Hamilton, 1955, p. 96.

22. '*Engineering* . . . deals with the conception, design, construction and application of new forms of equipment, machines or installations, and with ensuring the most efficient and economic means of achieving defined objectives by such means . . . An *Engineer* is the creator of projects of engineering significance, large or small, and it is his responsibility to bring together all the elements required to attain some prescribed objective. He frequently has to use the results and methods of different technologies . . . He has always to be the planner, and he may frequently be called upon to exercise managerial skills; he may on occasion have to be a financial expert or a financial entrepreneur. In every *Technology* the ultimate purpose is to exploit existing scientific and other knowledge for productive ends, whether or not all the processes involved in the technology are currently capable of scientific explanation. Examples are seen in chemical technology and in the technologies of materials (glass, textiles, plastics, rubber), processes (metallurgy and welding) and products (micro-electronic devices, water turbines). In this context, technology and engineering embody common attitudes . . . However, in method of approach, the processes of technology are frequently identical with those of the experimental sciences . . . The technologist is frequently several steps ahead of the scientist in the breadth of his knowledge and in his awareness of the potentialities within his field of enquiry, but he is likely to be less concerned with full understanding of the underlying scientific relationships.' *Report on the 1965 Manpower Survey* (note 12 to chapter 2), paragraphs 8 to 10.

Notes to Pages 155-157

23. A study by M. C. McCarthy has compared specialization in education and employment in Britain and the United States of America. 'Demand for specialists may be produced by technological or other factors, but may be most clearly identified with that for persons engaged on basic research. In both American and British manufacturing industry, the proportion of scientists and engineers employed in research and development has shown little movement, and future projections over the next ten years suggest no movement towards increased specialization. Present estimates show specialist requirements to be a maximum of 30 per cent of all science- and technology-based graduates' (M. C. McCarthy, *The Employment of Highly Specialized Graduates*, Department of Education and Science, Science Policy Studies No. 3, H.M.S.O., 1968, S.O. Code No. 27-418-3, Summary and Conclusions, p. v; I am grateful to the Secretariat of the Council for Scientific Policy for letting me have a copy before publication (cf. note 48 to chapter 3). The proportion of specialists emerging from the American educational system is of that order, but in Britain it is 85 per cent or more.

A second look shows what difficulties of definition and categorization are hidden under the broad statistics, but the general conclusion is unmistakable. Most American first degrees are generalist, most British ones are not. The major discrepancy between types of education and types of employment may lie at the root of some of the strains and stresses and disenchantments concerning the roles of qualified manpower in this country. McCarthy points out that, because of the emphasis on specialization in this country, 'generalist' tends to imply low calibre and he calls for 'the redemption of generalist courses from their present position of academic disrepute' ('The Highly Specialized Graduate', *Careers Research and Advisory Centre Journal* 3, pp. 5-8, 1968). In America, there is a category of 'high-level generalists' which includes the élite that goes on to one of the internationally renowned Business Schools after a first degree.

24. Bagrit (note 53 to chapter 3).

25. The proliferation of joint honours courses is partly a response to the call for more broadly based first degree courses made in the Robbins Report (*Higher Education*, Cmnd. 2154, H.M.S.O. 1963). As Anne Corbett comments in her useful survey

Notes to Pages 167-162

of the contents and fates of the major educational reports from 1959 to 1967 (*Much to do about education*, Council for Educational Advance, London, 1968, p. 18), the Robbins Report was not, however, primarily concerned with the content of its sector of the educational system, only with its structure.

26. For some views on what the science of science might or should consist of, see the book of that title edited by Goldsmith and Mackay (note 25 to chapter 2); the first annual lecture of the Science of Science Foundation, 'The Scientific Foundations of Science Policy', given by D. J. de Solla Price and printed in *Nature* 206, 233-8 (1965); and the second annual lecture by S. Dedijer, 'The Science of Science: A Programme and a Plea', printed in *Minerva* 4, 489-504 (1966). On the more humanistic aspects, an article by W. Mays, 'Teaching in the History and Philosophy of Science', *Nature* 208, 937-8 (1965), summarizes the results of a survey on the position in British and Irish universities, documenting 'consolidation rather than rapid advance' since 1960.

27. Cf. Krebs (note 14 to chapter 2). In addition there are less direct but also real ways in which the existence of a flourishing research school in an institution can help to raise the standard of undergraduate teaching—by attracting good staff and students and by keeping the former intellectually alive and the latter stimulated by a sense of contact with progress.

28. See note 30 to chapter 2.

29. One outspoken industrial critic of the Ph.D. system as now practised is Dr. D. S. Davies, formerly Laboratory Director of the large Petrochemicals and Polymers Laboratory of I.C.I.; see his article, 'The Chemistry of the Ph.D.—Industrial Dissatisfactions' in *The Times Educational Supplement*, October 7, 1966. It does seem to be the case that in terms of particular choices of research topics, of attitudes to problem-solving and of the motivation engendered, Ph.D. work in universities is often at cross-purposes with some major requirements of industry. See also sections 2f, 3g and 4b.

30. The proliferation of four-year undergraduate courses was officially discouraged by the Robbins Report (note 25 above).

31. A major difference between American and British higher

education is the 'full-time or nothing' attitude here, which in practice means relatively little university education after beginning employment. There is more than there was, but still not as much as there probably should be. McCarthy points out (note 23 above) that the American type of generalist first degree course followed by emphasis on in-career training helps to overcome problems of technological obsolescence and fosters closer contacts and better mutual understanding between universities and industry.

32. Even in more conventional situations, it is not uncommon for teachers to find themselves inhibited or hindered by knowing too much. Many teach best in areas of their subjects other than those in which their research activities lie.

33. M. Yudkin, 'The Place of Science in General Education', *The Oxford Review*, Hilary 1967, pp. 33-57.

34. An objection to courses on scientific method as commonly practised, though not an objection in principle, is that they tend to emphasize *differences* between science and other activities. Thus one might be told how Blake's 'O Rose, thou art sick!' and 'Tiger! Tiger! burning bright' differ from botany and zoology. Is it oversophisticated to suppose that differences between science and poetry are obvious enough and that it might be enlightening to probe their similarities as well for a change?

35. Conant (note 1 to chapter 2; see also note 55 to chapter 3). Detailed case history material has been published in J. B. Conant (editor), *Harvard Case Histories in Experimental Science*, Harvard University Press, 1964 (two volumes).

36. Yudkin's own prescription is for a laboratory-based course. My reservations about this type of solution are given in section 5f.

37. Conant does not ignore this but, having the scientific education of laymen principally in mind, he chooses not to emphasize it. 'The danger in the type of course I am suggesting will not be the danger of neglecting to put the case histories in their proper historical setting, but rather that the examination of the setting may take too much time. After all, I am suggesting a course in the Tactics and Strategy of Science, not one on European cultural history as illustrated by episodes in science, though the

Notes to Page 166

latter might be of value in the education of future scientists and engineers.' *On Understanding Science* (note 1 to chapter 2), p. 71.

38. It will be evident that I have strong personal views on the teaching of the history of science. A course which I give to students in the Department of Liberal Studies in Science in Manchester is based principally on the scientific revolution of the 16th and 17th centuries: Copernicus's proposal of a sun-centred universe, Galileo's efforts to achieve acceptance for it, Harvey's demonstration of the circulation of the blood and Bacon's vision of science applied for the welfare of mankind. This relatively restricted historical base is used to illuminate a number of general issues affecting science; indeed, the discussion concerns modern comment on the significance of the events as much as the events themselves. The issues raised include the origins of conceptual revolutions in science and the impact they may have on social institutions and accepted values; the aims and motivations of scientists; the patronage of science; the popularization of science; the social roles of science and the relations between scientists and statesmen; the status of scientific theories and the relation between theories and empirical facts; the roles of mathematical and experimental methods; and the places of logic and intuition in science.

INDEX

A level 101, 103, 110-12, 145, 184, 186, 200
abstraction 37
activity 41, 147
administration 121-3, 137, 188, 189, 193
all-rounders 108-9, 125, 128, 149, 191
anisotropy 52
applications 40, 52, 66-9, 74, 141, 149
applied science 34, 52, 54-5, 66-9, 86-92, 134-6, 154, 170, 204
apprenticeship 15, 25, 35-6, 39, 118
Armstrong A. 198
Armstrong H. E. 147
Ashby E. 91
Astryx 171, 190
atom bombs 74, 98, 124, 173, 182
Australia 124
autonomy 49, 51, 65

Bacon F. 61, 65-73, 75, 82, 88, 140, 172, 204
Baeyer A. von 35
Bagrit L. 97, 156
basic science 34, 52, 54-5, 86-92, 134-6, 170
Beard R. M. 174
Bellarmine R. 63
Bernal J. D. 74, 172
Bibby C. 174
biological organism model 49, 54
bisociation 45-8, 104
Blake W. 203
boarding need 191
books 24, 25, 33, 38-9, 41, 43, 141, 145, 148, 158
Bosworth Report 193
breadth 49, 114, 142, 184
Brierley J. K. 183
B.Sc. 118, 160
Business Schools 83, 137, 201
Butler J. R. 186

careers 17-19, 104-5, 132-8, 186, 198
Carter C. F. 96, 175, 179-80
Chesterton G. K. 27
Churchill W. 97

citations 24, 187
Civil Service 84-5, 97, 121-2, 156, 174, 188, 193
classics 43, 78, 81, 84, 109, 122, 143, 186
classification 115, 187
coherence 115-17, 149-51, 157-8
Conant J. B. 21, 80, 97, 164-5, 182, 203
concreteness 37-41, 47, 164
Confederation of British Industry 170, 192
convergers 108-9
Copernicus 44, 61-2, 71, 182, 204
Corbett A. 201
cost-effectiveness 13
Council for Scientific Policy 53, 170, 175, 201
creativity 44-9, 147-8
Crowther J. G. 172
Crowther Report 102, 107, 184-5, 190
cumulation 22-7, 110, 148

Dainton Report 10, 103, 107, 123-8, 142, 145, 183, 188, 191
Darwin C. 45, 165, 172
Davies D. S. 202
decision-making 82, 97, 122, 168, 181
degrees 48, 113, 117-20, 159, 161, 186
depth 48-9, 113-17, 151, 157, 158, 188
Descartes R. 21, 60
divergers 108-9, 191
Docksey P. 192
Dodd C. H. 122
Domar E. D. 175
Drake S. 171
Du Pont 90

economic growth 85-6, 98, 175
economics 154, 155
educational inertia 116, 129, 146, 152, 194
educators 20, 120, 131-2, 134, 138, 142, 144
Einstein A. 64
employment see careers
engineering 55, 77, 92, 93, 105, 110, 126, 134, 137, 154, 190, 200

205

entry requirements 101, 112, 113, 130
Evans W. G. 9, 175
Everest 15
evolution 15
examinations 44, 102, 135, 192-3
examining boards 112, 129-30, 139, 144, 184
expenditure on research 53, 86, 127, 170, 178
exponential growth 36, 109

facts 26, 30, 32-3, 47-8, 64, 79-82, 110-11, 140-1, 144, 153, 204
fallacy of misplaced concreteness 38, 164
fall-out 28, 59, 143
Faraday M. 75
Farrington B. 172
floating voters 125, 143
Flowers B. H. 9, 53
France 123, 124, 191
Franck Report 29
Freeman C. 179
Fulton Report 84, 188

Galileo Galilei 21, 23, 61-6, 72, 204
Gee G. 9
General Motors 87
general studies 101-2, 155, 163, 184
generalist activities 84, 121, 123
generalists 156, 189, 201
genetics 16, 64, 91, 167
Germany 64, 123, 124, 178
Geymonat L. 61
Gibbons M. 9, 175
Gilpin R. 28, 180-1
glorified plumbing 62, 66
Gradgrind fallacy 164
Greats 85, 115, 185
Gutenberg J. 45

Hardy G. H. 74
Harvey W. 21, 71, 73, 204
heat 70
history 43, 45, 60, 82, 83, 85, 109, 115, 121, 122, 143, 145, 186
history of science 42, 44-6, 60, 82, 156, 157, 164-6, 202, 204
Hogan W. P. 175
Hope F. 167
hour-glass theory 104, 107, 126
Hoyle F. 168
Hudson L. 108-9, 169
Hutchings D. 174, 185, 199

Huxley J. S. 171
Huxley T. H. 174
hypothetico-deductive method 30-1, 64, 71

I.C.I. 87, 202
inductive method 30, 70-1, 172
industry 87-90, 92-7, 100, 119, 178-80, 134-7, 201, 203
inertial bias 125
information explosion 110
innovation 86, 89, 175, 178
input-output analysis 13
integrating functions 93, 97-9, 127, 154, 158
integration 149-52, 157
inventions 67, 95, 179
investigational method 41, 147
invisible hand 50
Irvine W. 174

James, Walter 174
James, William 109
Japan 55
Jennings A. H. 191
Jevons F. R. 168, 171, 173, 180, 182, 187
Jewkes J. 179
Johnson S. 102
joint honours 155, 157, 163, 201
journalism 77, 163, 173
Jung C. G. 109
Jungk R. 168

knowledge pressure 109, 111
Knowlson P. M. 192
Koestler A. 31, 44-5, 61, 142
Krebs H. A. 36, 168-9, 202
Krenke N. P. 91
Kuhn T. S. 38, 44-6, 182

Langrish J. 9, 175, 176, 180
law 65, 154, 189-90
Lawrence D. H. 125
lectures 42, 138, 140, 148, 161, 194, 196-7, 198
Liberal Studies in Science 9, 175, 180, 194, 204
licences 176
Liebig J. 36
Lighthill M. J. 191
Lilienthal 29
Lipson H. S. 177
Locke J. 21, 115
logic 31, 63-4, 108, 204

INDEX

McCarthy M. C. 201, 203
McLeish J. 198
Mallory G. 15
management 83, 88, 93-4, 96-7, 105, 124, 127, 134, 137-8, 154-5, 193
Manchester 9, 116, 194
manpower 19, 76, 87, 93, 127, 171, 176, 177, 201
Margolis J. 187
marketing 83, 88, 94
mathematics 28, 46, 64, 74, 83, 108, 121, 125, 126, 128, 136, 187, 191, 198, 204
Mays W. 10, 202
Medawar P. B. 34, 110, 169
memorization 40, 42, 82, 140
Mendel G. 64, 91
Merchants of Light 68, 90
Merton R. K. 51-2, 169
Metcalfe S. 175
molecular biology 76, 111, 115, 173
Morgan T. H. 64
motivation 38, 57, 59, 88-91, 105, 135, 204
Mueller W. F. 176
multiple exemplification 114
multispecialist 49, 156, 162
Murray G. 10, 196

nature-story 32-44, 79, 140, 145, 153, 164
Needham J. 51
Netherlands 123, 124
Newton I. 21, 22
Nobel prizes 34, 35, 55, 103, 106, 128, 173
nuclear physics 75-6, 92
Nuffield 199, 200
numeracy 82-3, 185
numeracy barrier 121, 127, 128

O level 101, 123, 183, 186
Occam W. 144
organization 35, 68, 115

paradigm 44
patents 95, 179
personality 125, 134-5, 146
Peter Pan complex 74, 162
Peterson A. D. C. 184
Ph.D. 35, 89, 106, 118, 160, 202
philanthropy 58, 66, 131
planning 68, 72, 83, 88, 94, 154
Plato 32, 34, 149
Polanyi M. 25, 31, 50

politics 28-9, 65, 72-3, 97, 100, 173, 180-1, 189
Pope A. 77, 184
Popper K. 31, 62
popularization 77-8, 204
positivism 62
postgraduate work 118, 159-62
practical work 41, 146-9
prestige 38, 68, 84, 86, 89, 90, 112, 129, 155, 176
Price D. J. de Solla 36, 86, 109, 187
Price D. K. 97, 156
principles 47, 81
priority 38
production 83, 88, 94
profit 58
progress 21-7, 110, 130
projects 113
psychological considerations 44, 104, 106-9
Pullman W. A. 190
pure science *see* basic science
push and pull models 170, 180

reading 41, 82, 140-6, 148, 157, 162, 193, 194-8
research front 25, 77, 82, 89, 100, 118-20, 152-4, 187
research and development 86, 88, 93-5, 170, 178, 180, 182, 201 (*see also* expenditure)
Robbins Report 201, 202
Rose S. P. R. 169
Rothman H. 9
Rowe A. P. 91
Royal Society 51, 66, 127
Russia 64, 91, 177

Salomon's House 68
Sawers D. 179
Scherer F. M. 170
Schmookler J. 179
scholarship 18, 81, 114, 129, 133
scholasticism 63
Schools Council 103, 129, 184, 185, 188
Science Greats 9, 116, 194, 204
science of science 157, 166, 202
science policy 72, 86, 127, 157, 170, 176, 202
scientific method 27-31, 63-4, 164, 203
science-oriented humanist 156, 162
Scotland 183, 191
separability 96
Shakespeare W. 59

Shaw G. B. 41
sixth form 101-3, 123-6, 128-30, 145, 150-1, 184
skill mix 95-6
Smith A. 50
Snow C. P. 98
social science 83, 124, 183, 186, 189
sociology of science 157, 166, 169
Solow R. 175
specialists 71, 96-8, 121, 128, 143, 149, 189, 201
specialization 18, 25, 98-130, 133, 162, 188, 192
Spencer H. 32
Spice J. 200
spin-off 28, 59
Stein G. 122
Stillerman R. 179
style 120, 139-44, 145, 194-8
subject boundaries 114-15, 151, 187
subject-mindedness 107, 112, 190
Swann Report 54, 160, 171, 182
swing from science 16, 27, 123-8, 143
syllabuses 101, 125, 139, 144-6, 147, 150-1, 152, 200

technique 34, 38, 46
technocrats 190
technology 52, 59-60, 85-90, 126, 134, 136, 190, 200
technology transfer 90, 136, 154
theology 65, 126
theories 26, 30, 32-3, 47-8, 64, 69, 110-11, 204
Thomson J. J. 198
traditions 23-4, 35

United States of America 87, 101, 106, 163-4, 173, 175, 179, 182, 184, 201, 203

values 51, 65, 204
vocational education 13, 18, 84, 117, 121, 124, 133-4, 186, 188-9

Waddington C. H. 167
Watson J. D. 142
Weinberg A. M. 77, 173
Weismann A. 64
Whitehead A. N. 38, 40
Wilde O. 88
Williams B. R. 96, 175, 176, 179-80
Wren-Lewis J. 190

Yudkin M. 163, 203

Ziman J. M. 167, 173
Zirkle C. 171

Printed and bound by CPI Group (UK) Ltd, Croydon, CR0 4YY
24/07/2024
01020826-0003